FROM GROSS SPIRITUAL DARKNESS
To
GLORIOUS HEAVENLY LIGHT

FROM GROSS SPIRITUAL DARKNESS
To
GLORIOUS HEAVENLY LIGHT

YEAR 1923

To

YEAR 2020

JOURNEY WITH ME THROUGH THE TWENTIETH CENTURY

BY
DR. RALPH J. MCINTYRE

XULON PRESS

Xulon Press
2301 Lucien Way #415
Maitland, FL 32751
407.339.4217
www.xulonpress.com

Paperback ISBN-13: 978-1-6312-9645-1

ACKNOWLEDGMENTS

I have truly been blessed and encouraged by so many people as I re-traveled the winding road of my life, recalling the past and recording the many different happenings of my four generations in this book: *"From Gross Spiritual Darkness to Glorious Heavenly Light."* I extend my sincere appreciation to everyone that has prompted me with their many comments. I give special thanks to the following that have assisted me throughout this endeavor.

Reverend Terry McIntyre, my son, truly provoked me one day when he said, *"Dad, with so many different changes that have taken place during your life of many years, there is probably much of your life that I know nothing about. If you could put all the past that you can remember in a book, it would be a real blessing to me and to others."* He went on to say, *"I would be happy to proofread and edit the book for you."* He has been true to his word by taking time out of his very busy schedule, applying many long hours and completing this remarkable deed. His inspiration and suggestions have been treasurable.

Karen Cole, my daughter, and her husband, Reverend Steve Cole, have opened their home unto me and treated me royally. I have visited with them several months at a time in their home. I have used their computer over many hours to write this book, and was given free reign to whatsoever I needed. My daughter was a great help to me in every way.

David Toft, a true Christian and dear friend, has spent countless hours assisting me in many different ways. He has always been available for anything that I needed at any time, and has readily come to my assistance at a moment's notice. I still have the assurance that I can call upon David at any time for anything. He has always given tremendous help to me and encouraged me in so many ways. He keeps my computer in good operating condition, and he cropped and copied the pictures in proper form for this book.

DEDICATION

My Family

To my beloved (deceased) wife, Frances, for the love, faith and kindness she so lavishly gave. She was my constant companion for over sixty-three years. She gave me much strength and encouragement. Proverbs chapter thirty-one describes her perfectly.

To my son, Reverend Terry B. McIntyre, and his wife, Lynda, Missionaries in Africa and Fiji in the South Pacific

To my daughter, Karen, and her husband, Reverend Steve Cole, Pastor in Athens, Georgia

To my granddaughter, Tawana, and her husband, Reverend Scott Richardson, Pastor in Baltimore (Essex), Maryland and their children: Tristan and Taylor

To my grandson, Terry Blaine McIntyre, Jr., residing in Baltimore (Towson), Maryland

To my grandson, Dale Cole, and his wife, Beverly, and their children: Ethyn, Gavin, and Emma residing in Atlanta (Douglasville), Georgia

To my grandson, Dane Cole, and his wife, Cherise, and their children: Jade and Jagur residing in Atlanta (Fayetteville), Georgia

To Pastor David Reever and Abundant Life Church of Baltimore, Maryland

To Pastor Steve Cole and the First Pentecostal Church of Athens, Georgia.

TABLE OF CONTENTS

COMMENTS

Dear Dr. McIntyre—

What a delightful story to edit–very inspiring and pro-
viding such an insight into the various generational changes
that have occurred throughout your lifetime (as well as the
intrinsic sets of human values that have in fact remained
the same).

Best regards,
Tara, editor

My Dear Dad, Dr. Ralph McIntyre—

It has been a joy of mine to proofread and refine your book. I
have learned things about you and our family that until now
I never knew. It has been a very enlightening and interesting
experience to read stories of your amazing life that takes me
back to my roots.

All my best always,

Terry McIntyre, proofreader/editor

AUTHOR'S NOTE

I've constructed dialogue from memory, which means it may not be word for word. But, the essence is accurate. When God breathes the breath of life into us, we become a living soul inside a human (physical) body. From day one, we need loving care and guidance.

My parents were good upright parents that believed there was a God and loved their children, but they were not active Christians. However, later as a gospel minister, I was blessed to be able to baptize my mother as you will discover later in this book.

In 1930 at my age of seven, we discovered very early on Christmas morning that my father had passed away some time during the night from a heart attack. He was only thir-ty-seven years old. So, in my maturing years, I knew very little about God.

Without spiritual training during the times of youth, most essence, concerns and desires are directed upon the temporal instead of the eternal. I believed there was a God from things I had heard and seen, but I did not know how to find Him. Later, when God opened my spiritual eyes, I began to see the light of truth. God's Word gives us insight in Psalms 19:1-3 (NIV) where it states, *"The heavens declare the glory of God; the skies proclaim the work of His hands. Day after day they pour forth speech; night after night they display knowledge. There is no speech or language where their voice is not heard."*

As I grew into my teenage years, I attended several tent meetings. I liked the singing, but I did not understand the preaching. At the conclusion of the services, I witnessed people being instructed to raise their hands and accept the Lord as their Savior. Then, the preacher told them they were now Christians and saved. I did not know the Scriptures, but I did not believe that was the truth. I believed there was more to salvation than this.

Without proper direction, I continued traveling the road of sin for the first twenty-nine years of my life until God in His love and care miraculously called me out of darkness, rescued me from the path of destruction, opened my spiritual blind eyes and, eventually, anointed me to be a minister of the gospel to preach in the Apostolic church that Jesus is building.

I am very thankful for all of the people that I have been privileged to minister to and help guide in their spiritual walk during my sixty-four years in the ministry. They know who they are, and I hope they know they will always have my continuing love and deep appreciation.

PREFACE

The events transcribed in this book are all true and recounted from the best of my memory. My heart's desire is to share with the reader an insight into the various generational changes that have occurred throughout my lifetime of travel through the twentieth century, and continue to change as I continue my travels in the twenty-first century (to date) with the human values that have remained unchanged.

Motivation for engaging in this documentation of my life's story came about due to the encouragement of family members, fellow ministers and friends. At the outset, my approach to this project was with considerable reservation, yet I felt deep within my heart and a strong urging in my spirit that, in all fairness, I truly owed this to my children, grandchildren, great-grandchildren and many friends.

After meditating for a period of time, memories long forgotten began to resurface. I began making a list of these happenings of the days of yore. I was surprised to see how fast the list began to grow.

As I began to reminisce on my life from its inception, David's words came to me, as recorded in Psalm. 51:5 (NIV), *"Surely I was sinful at birth, sinful from the time my mother conceived me."* This enlightened me to the fact that everyone has their weak points, and no one is impeccable; whereas, I was refreshed in memory of my walk on the road of sin for the first twenty-nine years of my life. It was truly the road of "gross spiritual darkness."

During this period of time, although I did not know God, He knew me and He knew where I was at all times. God can take the vilest sinner and change them into a saint. People only see the visible side of humanity, but God looks upon the heart. The Scripture tells us that the heart is wicked and the purpose of Jesus coming to this earth was to give us a new heart as stated in Ezekiel 11:19-20 (NIV), *"I will give them an undivided heart and put a new spirit in them; I will remove from them their heart of stone and give them a heart of flesh. Then they will follow my decrees and be careful to keep my laws. They will be my people, and I will be their God."*

My wife and I were introduced to the "Light of the world," Jesus Christ our Lord, in May of 1953. This came about due to the caring saints of God that fasted and prayed for our family. We were baptized in water by immersion in the name of Jesus Christ to have our sins remitted, and later we both received the baptism of the Holy Spirit just like those people in the upper room as recorded in the Bible in Acts chapter two. This is what takes place in a person when he or she becomes a truly born-again Christian. Old things pass away, and all things become new. Gross darkness fled and glorious light shone brightly in our lives.

.Isaiah 60:1-2: (NIV) states *"Arise, shine, for your light has come, and the glory of the Lord rises upon you. See, darkness covers the earth, and thick darkness is over the peoples, but the Lord rises upon you and his glory appears over you."* Thus, my title for this document: **"From Gross Spiritual Darkness to Glorious Heavenly Light."**

I have endeavored to share my life's history as truthfully and honorably as humanly possible. Over the years, many things have grown quite vague, while some would be repetitive and others redundant. A young man in our church congregation by the name of Allen Campbell would respond to the ministered Word of God by saying, *"Tell it like it is!"* That is the axiom that I have endeavored to adhere to.

It is impossible to remember many of those happenings of yesteryear; nevertheless, I have tried seriously to give it my best. I trust that whosoever gives this document a review will enjoy the contents and be blessed.

During my research and recall, it was, at times, as though I was reliving and experiencing my life all over again. As the past began to resurface in my mind, some of the happenings were quite humorous and brought smiles while others created sadness and brought tears.

One of those humorous times was when my sister, Lorene, and I visited friends and were walking home on a very dark night. The country road leading to our house passed by a family cemetery. There was a very large oak tree in the corner where the road made a ninety degree turn to the left. Just as we made the turn, suddenly, just over our heads, there was a loud noise and a swishing sound.

Lorene was always very fast on her feet, but this night she soon almost lost sight of me. When I realized that an owl had dived down out of that tree, flapped its wings and squawked over our heads, I stopped and waited for my sister to catch up with me. When she got close, she said, *"A real protector you are!"* Well, there are just times in life when certain things happen that will cause an individual to react "on the spur of the moment." At times this goes against the norm.

I am not sorry to have recalled my past that I remembered. In fact, I am thankful that I was provoked to backpedal into my past life. At the finish, I found it refreshing. As humans, we are prone to forget much of which we need to remember and remember much of which we need to forget. Throughout this project, I was aided by the Holy Spirit and the deeply appreciated love and understanding of my family.

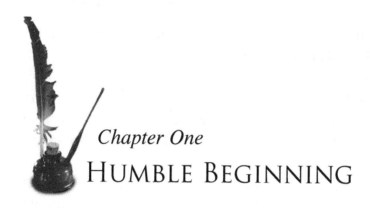

Chapter One

HUMBLE BEGINNING

In Rutherford County, located in the rolling hills of Western North Carolina, on November 13th, 1897, a daughter was born into the family of William Pickney and Lennie Ellen (Ledford) Towery, who decided on the name Dessie Bell.

When this child grew to school age, she attended Piedmont grade and high school, which was a three-mile walk each way. The only time her parents would permit her to go to school was when Essie, her sister, was able to go. However, Essie was sickly for much of her young life and had to miss many days of school. Therefore, Dessie had to miss, also. The only school education she was able to get occurred between the ages of seven and nine, which was not sufficient enough to learn to read or write.

At the age of nine she went to work at Cleveland Mills (a cotton mill). She was so short that she had to stand on a wood crate in order to reach her work. Her job included taking off full bobbin cones and replacing them with empty bobbins. When they were spinning sometimes the thread would break, and she would have to repair the thread. She worked from six in the morning until six in the evening for a very measly salary. After she had worked at this mill for one year, this mill closed. Then she went to work for a Major Shank at another mill, where they paid her only half her former pay.

At the age of eleven, Dessie's family moved to Double Shoals, North Carolina. Dessie went to work in a mill there. In those early days, there was no law against juvenile labor. Dessie's mother and father hated the fact that she had to quit school and go to work in a cotton mill.

At the age of thirteen, her mother wanted her to go back to school, but she refused, feeling that she was too old. Nevertheless, she was determined to get an education. There were four or five people at the mill that took turns teaching her for two hours on two different nights each week. Dessie was so anxious to learn to read that she would ask any girl that came along to write something down on a piece of paper in order that she could copy and learn it. By applying herself, she was able to learn to read and write quite well. On the other hand, I have very few details about the childhood of my father, Summie Jackson McIntyre.

Summie Jackson McIntyre and Dessie Towery met each other in Wadesboro, North Carolina, and they continued to enjoy each other's company for an extended period of time. Dessie was living in the country with her sister, Essie, and her husband, Jim Bracket. She was removing hulls from green walnuts on Saturday, August 16th, 1916, when Summie unexpectedly arrived. He informed her that his purpose for being there was to see if she would agree to marry him if they could find a minister to perform the ceremony.

There was a church across the road from the house of her brother, William, and it so happened that they were having a special service that afternoon. Summie went across to the church and spoke to Reverend J. W. Suttle. The minister returned with Summie and performed the wedding on the front porch of the house of Dessie's brother. He, then, pronounced Summie McIntyre and Dessie Towery husband and wife. **This couple became my Father and Mother.**

After the wedding, the couple stayed with Summie's parents for a week. Summie had left home at the age of eighteen. He traveled to South Carolina where he got into the lumber business. Leaving his parents' home, the newlyweds boarded a train and traveled south to Parkville, South Carolina. Wherever the heavy timber was located was where they would live.

Summie ran the mill and kept the books. Every time all of the trees were cleared in an area, the mill had to be moved to another area causing dad to have to find another place to move the family to. It was always another primitive house.

Family Growth

Mother gave birth to a baby girl on April 14th, 1917 in Parkville, South Carolina, which was located in McCormick County before the doctor was able to arrive. When Doctor Blackwell did arrive, my mother was hemorrhaging very badly and without him, she would probably have died. Afterwards, she was bedfast for nine days before she could sit up. The name chosen for this baby was Vertie Aselee, but, unfortunately, she developed boils and an abscess on the brain and only lived for two months, passing away on June 14th, 1917, which was Dad's birthday.

Several years later on December 21st, 1920 in Gibson, Georgia, which was located in Glascock County, the second daughter was born just prior to midnight in a sawmill shack in the middle of the woods. Doctor Mitchell delivered her into the world. The name given to this second daughter was Lorene Bennett.

At approximately eleven o'clock on Saturday morning, August 18th, 1923, Summie Jackson and Dessie McIntyre became the parents of their first son. This birth took place in Double Branch, Georgia, which was a small community north of Augusta, Georgia located in Lincoln County and bordering the South Carolina line.

In those days, not many people could afford the luxury of a hospital; therefore, the birth of their third child took place in their humble home with the assistance of the local mid-wife. Parents usually chose names for both male and female children, because they had to wait until the child arrived before determining the gender. Ralph Jackson was chosen as the first and middle names for this healthy baby boy, **who is the author expressing from memory the happenings in this book.**

Some years later, on the afternoon of November 12th, 1926, near Red Hill, South Carolina, located in Edgefield County, the second son was born into the family. On her way to aid in the birth, a mid-wife by the name of Aunt Necie stumbled over a foot log and fell into the creek. She wasn't hurt, but everyone thought it was funny, because her dress rose up and exposed her flour sack underwear.

Dad was sent for, arrived on horseback and went into Red Hill to get the doctor. Doctor Whitlock was out of town on another call, but dad was able to get a new doctor by the name of Bush to come and deliver the baby. They named this son Roy Lee.

Between 2:00 PM and 6:00 PM on Saturday, December 28th, 1929, in McCormick County near Modoc, South Carolina, another daughter was born into the McIntyre family before the doctor arrived. A lady by the name of Mrs. Smalley washed the baby and discovered a large birthmark on her head. The doctor arrived, and Mrs. Smalley showed him the birthmark.

Mother wanted to know if something was wrong with the baby. The doctor assured her that it was just a birth mark and that everything was fine. The name chosen this time was Ellen Evalina. This completed all of the members of our McIntyre family.

As children, in those early years, we were loved and cared for, but it was impossible to get the attention that families today extend to their children. We never got any toys, but we never missed the things that we did not have. The most important thing shared in a family is genuine love and care. Our parents loved all of us children and did their best for us with what they had.

Back in those days most everyone believed in God, but they did not know Him. Therefore, many families were non-church attendees. My parents were in that group.

Dad's Work and Family Life

Felling Trees for Sawmill

At the sawmill dad's duties required long days, hard work and little pay. But, dad was thankful to have a job and never complained. When they finished cutting all of the trees in one area, the mill had to be moved to another area. This took several days to accomplish. The workers stayed in makeshift barracks and mother was overseer in preparing the meals.

All of the houses we lived in were quite primitive. There was no electricity or inside plumbing. In the winter time, heating was derived from the kitchen wood stove and fireplaces. At one house we lived in, the water supply came from a spring that was about one-third of a mile from the house. There was a path through a thick wooded area that led to this spring.

Monday was usually designated as laundry day, weather permitting, which took place at the spring location. There was a large black wash pot under which a fire was built in order to boil the clothes, and a large wood paddle was used to stir them, which loosened up the dirt and soil. After boiling them, the clothes were placed in galvanized wash tubs and scrubbed by hand on a wash board, rinsed, wrung out by hand, (as wringers were unheard of in the days of yore), and hung on lines stretched from tree to tree to dry.

Laundry day was just another opportunity for Roy and me to strip off to our birthday suit and catch bullfrogs in the creek that the spring fed into. We were quite successful catching these frogs. In fact, later in life, Roy declared me as the champion frog catcher. All of the family enjoyed feasting on the frog legs. Occasionally, in the summer, our family had a lot of fun in a swimming hole located there, also.

The Savannah River ran close by our house. Dad placed several fish baskets into the river and baited them in order to catch catfish. I loved to go to the river with dad to collect the fish, but there were a couple of things that made me hesitant. There was a long bottom land to cross, and it had a weed called a stinging nettle. When this weed brushed against you, it made you feel like a swarm of bees had landed on you. Another drawback was a bridge that crossed the river, and the boards were about two or three inches apart causing a young boy to feel for sure that he was going to fall through one of those cracks and wind up in the river.

In October of 1929 the Great Depression began, and banks suddenly padlocked their doors. They had run out of money due to the heavy withdrawal. This brought a very heavy hardship on everyone suddenly and unexpectedly.

Highways of our nation were filled with men searching for jobs. They were not like the typical tramps of the years before the Great Depression. They were young men who had just graduated from high school or college and should have been looking forward to a bright future. There were older men who were experienced in a trade and hard work, and some men who had at one time been successful in careers or business.

With millions of people out of work, many families had to start over, move on or find a new way to earn a living. Now, many of them were searching for any job to be found. When all banks closed, there were a number of men that lost everything. They were now penny wise. Sad, but true, this sudden shock caused some men to wind up taking their own lives. I was six years of age when these hardship days began.

Hobos Came from All Walks of Life

The 1930's were the toughest years in history, especially since there were no jobs to be had—not even the farmers were hiring. Thousands of people (hobos) rode boxcars from place to place in hopes of earning a few pennies. Sometimes, when there weren't any boxcars to ride in, people rode on top of the trains no matter what the weather was like. Hopping a freight train was dangerous, but for those without money, it was an inexpensive way to travel in search of work.

Hobos, also, had to be on the watch for railroad detectives. If they were caught, they wound up in jail with no money in order to pay a fine. Therefore, they spent sentenced time in jail.

On top of all that, there were the great droughts of 1934 through 1936. Due to the hot sun burning out the heartland, entire states were turned into the Dust Bowl.

Our house in South Carolina was very near to the railroad. Therefore, we saw a lot of hobos. They got a day's work on occasion, and then, sent a dollar or two back home to their families. Some hobos would stop by our house to ask for something to eat. At times, they would offer to chop wood or perform any other type of work in exchange for food. Many would say, *"Just a biscuit or two or anything left from your meal will be fine, ma'am."* Hobos always came to the back door, never the front door. Dad and mom had agreed that anyone that asked for a bite to eat would never be refused.

I'm happy that I had the privilege of living and experiencing life during that period of time. Although during this period of time life was truly harsh, it taught me a lesson that has stuck with me all through my life—that is, material things aren't the important things in life. As these tough times enveloped the nation, folks began to see their neighbors in a new and more loving light.

When the banks closed, hearts were opened. People came to the realization that they were not an island or a loner, but a community that truly needed each other. No one who lived through the Great Depression can forget the terrible toll it took on the whole nation. Those who survived remember the hard times too well, but are more likely to speak of the courage, strength and love that saw them through.

Close Call

When I was about five years of age, there was a storage building behind the house where we lived. One day Lorene, Roy and I were playing in this building when I climbed up and retrieved a tin can from a top shelf. Upon opening it, the contents appeared to be a sweet syrup. About the only time we got any candy or sweets was at Christmas time and that was a very limited amount; therefore, anything sweet certainly appealed to us. Roy and I began eating it until Lorene saw what we were doing and yelled, *"Don't eat that!"* and tossed the can into a patch of weeds.

When we went into the house, our observant mother noticed a sticky substance on Roy's overalls, which Lorene had tried to clean off. She questioned Lorene who said, *"I don't know what it was, Mother, but when I saw them eating it, I grabbed it up and tossed it into the weeds."* Mother smelled it and realized it was bean spray syrup that you mix with water and spray for bean beetles. This bean spray contained arsenic. An elderly lady had owned this house near Parkville, South Carolina, and she had thrown away some arsenic, but overlooked this can on the top shelf. Mom threw dad his hat, and he went to get Doctor Blackwell.

When they returned, the doctor instructed dad to bring in a washtub from the back porch. He then proceeded to give both of us a small amount (about the size of a dime) of something that looked like gun powder, castor oil and egg white. In a short time, Roy was sick and bent over the washtub gagging. I was sitting there, and the doctor said, *"Ralph, aren't you sick?"* I said, *"Yes, sir, but I am trying not to vomit!"* He said, *"That boy!"* He proceeded to give me another dose, which certainly put an end to my holding power. Everyone was thankful that Roy, who was only three years of age and naturally kind of sloppy, had dropped some of the syrup onto the bib of his overalls. The doctor said, *"It is a good thing that arsenic works slowly."* It was the early observance of our mother that saved our lives.

Small Flame Starts Big Fire

Another time, Lorene, Roy and I were playing in the woods, and I had brought along some matches. We got the bright idea to build ourselves a fire. Everything was very dry and when the fire got to burning good, it spread to the dry pine needles. We tried to put the fire out, but it wasn't long until it was completely out of control. We had to run to get out of the woods, because the fire was moving very fast. If we dared to let our parents know how that fire had started, there would have been more than those woods burning and rightly so.

A large gang of men quickly assembled to combat that fire, which burned through a very large area before being brought under control and extinguished. After investigation, all of those men agreed that the fire was started by sparks coming from one of the freight trains as it passed through the area. We never tried repeating that stunt again.

Work, Mischief and Play

Lorene and I had the responsibility every evening of carrying the needed water supply from the spring to the house. One day, we were playing big time and forgot all about this duty. When dad came home and found no water, he was very angry. Although darkness had set in, we still had to go to the spring and fetch the water.

You talk about being frightened...our imagination told us there was a wild animal behind every tree or a ghost hovering close by ready to grab us. (People told a lot of ghost stories in those days, and we children believed them). Also, every stick we stepped on caused us to know it just had to be a snake. Unknown to us until years later, our mother had followed us close enough to make sure we were alright.

Roy was fascinated with terrapins or land turtles. He found one in the woods and brought it home, but didn't know what to do with it. Thinking it needed to be in water, he put it in the water bucket that contained our drinking water. When mother saw that turtle in the bucket, she went bananas! Finding out which one of us had done this deed she said, *"Young man, you are going to get a good thrashing."*

Roy took off running, but underestimated mom's running ability. He stayed a good way in front of her until he had to cross a low fence. He made it across the fence just fine, but when he started to continue his run, he stumbled and fell. Mom just sailed right over that fence and caught him. We knew mom kept her word, because Roy could be heard yelling.

Mom and Roy came back to the house together, and mom scrubbed and scalded the water bucket. Since the water bucket was now empty, the water brigade, (you know who), had to go to the spring for fresh water. When dad came home, he was ready to give Roy another switching, but mom convinced him that she had done a proper job.

We moved again to a place which had a front porch that ran the width of the house. The steps were being replaced and a very sharp stake stood beside the steps. When I was running and playing on this porch, I fell on this stake which stuck into my face, barely missing my left eye. The pressure from the stake caused my eyeball to pop out of its socket. Dad almost fainted and had to lay down on the porch for a while. He, then, went into the small community and once again returned with the country doctor.

When the doctor looked at the eye, he said, *"I think we can fix this and make it work again."* He took his rough hands and popped the eyeball back into place and said, *"Well, I think everything will be alright now."* Although a scar remained, that eye never caused me any problems, and I retained a perfect 20–20 vision until much later in life when I grew older.

School Days Begin

Lorene was two years and eight months older than me, but dad would not let her start school until I reached the age of six to go with her. So, in 1929, we both entered the first grade at the Washington Consolidated High School, which had no inside plumbing.

One day, some boys grabbed my new sweater and threw it down in the outside toilet. I went crying to Lorene, and she was very thankful that it happened to land where she could fish it out. After she got through with those boys, I wasn't bothered by them again. We thought it was best not to tell dad, because he would have gone to the school and, perhaps, caused some trouble.

Some of the teachers taught more than one class in the same room together. They would teach one grade, and then move over to the next grade. Thankfully, at the end of the school year, we were both promoted to the second grade. Instead of me looking out for Lorene's welfare, it was the other way around. She was my guardian angel, as she would not let others run over her brother.

In 1930, things began to get really tough, financially, due to the depression that had struck the year before. Dad told mom that he did not have the money to buy what was needed for that school year; therefore, we were not able to go back to school that fall.

Dad was working twelve to fourteen hours every day, but due to the crash of the banks and the setting in of the Great Depression of 1929, his salary was truly meager. Dad and mom were both very worried and regretful, especially for Lorene, because she was already ten years of age. However, they could see no way to enroll us in school for the second year. In fact, there was hardly any money for food.

Lorene and I would see other children going to school, and we felt bad that we could not go also, because we both liked going to school. It was not possible for our mother to home-school us, because she had not been able to get enough education to enable her to teach us.

The house where we lived had been built during the slave days, and it was beginning to show its age. There was even a slave cemetery behind the house. This house was built on a slope and set on pillars that raised it up between two and three feet off the ground, which provided an opening underneath. We were permitted to live there rent free, because no one knew who owned the property. There were no glass windows; instead, the windows were made of lumber and were on hinges, so you could open them in the summer time to get some fresh air.

Replica of My Friend, Billie

I had a goat named "Billie." On one hot day, my mother had opened the windows to let the fresh air flow in. Old Billie spotted the opening and leaped in through the opened window. He was in the middle of the bed looking into a large mirror, twisting his head from side to side and probably trying to figure out that goat that he was looking at. My mother walked into the bedroom with a broom in her hand. When she saw Billie, she took a swing at him. Needless to say, old Billie wasted no time going back out that window.

Dad had a stripped-down T-model Ford, and one day he came home with a small red wagon tied onto the back of it.

Lorene said, *"Daddy, where did you get that?"* Dad informed us that as soon as he had time, he would hook old Billie to the wagon and let us take a ride.

Truly, that was the wrong message for a curious young boy. I was excited about that venture, and I just couldn't wait—the suspense was too great. I begged my mother to hook up Billie, but she told me to wait on my father. But, one day I hooked Billie up by myself without any lines to guide him. I jumped into the wagon and yelled, *"Go Billie!"* — and, go he did!

As Billie headed out, the noise scared him. This caused him to pick up speed and run toward the opening under the house. If he had made it, my head would have been smashed; but, fortunately for me, that accident was avoided, because just before that would have happened, Billie made a slight turn and flipped the wagon over spilling me out onto the ground. Thank God, all I got were some scratches and bruises.

When dad came home and heard the story of my venture, he went out and hitched Billie up to the wagon. Then, he ordered me to get into the wagon, which reluctantly I did, but this time everything went off smoothly.

Subsidizing Wages with Illegal Activity

Dad worked six days a week for very small wages and had a family of six to provide for. Dad, on occasion, in order to supplement his salary, would make a run of pure corn whiskey, which was better known as white lightning or moonshine. One of the men who worked for dad got angry with him and reported him to the sheriff's office for selling illegal liquor. No member of our household would ever forget the day when the sheriff and a carload of deputies pulled in to make a raid of our home place.

Most everyone was scared silly except dad, who remained very calm. After they had covered seemingly every inch of our property and found no alcoholic beverage, they left satisfied. A very short time later, one of dad's customers came to purchase some of the product. Dad told him just to wait a few moments. Dad went out the back door, and in a few minutes returned with the customer's order. To this day, it remains a mystery as to where dad's hiding place was.

On another day dad and the crew were off work for some reason, and several of them had joined up to have a few social drinks. One of the men who worked for dad needed a knife, and dad loaned him his pocket knife. They all seemed to be having a pleasant time until dad and the man that had borrowed his knife got into a disagreement that began to heat up.

When dad started to walk away, the man stabbed him in the side with his own knife. The knife went rather deep into his side, but dad refused to go to the doctor. So, mom gathered some soot from the fireplace (as it was sterile) and packed the wound with the soot to stop the bleeding. This treatment worked, and dad was fine after the soreness went away. Meanwhile, all of us children had really been frightened and had run from the house. We hid in a ravine until mother called out to us stating that everything was all right.

Over Indulging

On Sunday mornings it was customary in this household to have breakfast a little later than usual. On this particular Sunday, after the food was prepared and everyone was at the table, dad informed us children that he had a little surprise for us later on. We were excited, anxious and could hardly wait.

Finally, mom brought in a bowl of blackberries, which was a welcome treat. Then, dad went to a closet and brought out a half-gallon of his white lightening — boy, were we surprised when dad poured a small amount of the whiskey over our berries. Honestly, all confessed that it did taste quite good.

After breakfast, mom and dad went to the barn to catch a chicken for dinner. Meanwhile, I went back into the kitchen and got another bowl of those blackberries. Then, I went to the closet, got the jar of whiskey and poured quite a sum of it over my berries. I replaced the jar of whiskey back in the closet and proceeded to enjoy my feast. By the time I had finished eating them and being only six years of age, my head had begun to swim. I walked out onto the front porch as my parents were returning from the barn with the chicken and yelled, *"Whoopee! I'm drunk."* Dad said to mom, *"Look at that boy acting the fool, because I gave him a little taste of whiskey."*

There were six steps at the front of the house. I took one step, rolled down the last five and was out like a light. Dad picked me up, carried me in the house and placed me on the bed. Then, he went and checked his whiskey jar. He came back and told mom, *"That little devil has gone back into the closet and gotten into that whiskey. He really is drunk."*

I didn't wake up from my stupor until around two o'clock in the afternoon. My mother had fixed some chicken and dumplings and asked me if I was hungry. I said, *"No mother. I'm sick."* I never tried that caper again during my childhood.

Chapter Two

HAPPY TIMES
AND SAD TIMES

E arly on Christmas morning of 1929, the McIntyre children were awakened to music. Jumping out of bed, we
ran to see where it was coming from. Dad had bought a phono-
graph and was playing a record, which was an amazing feature
we had never seen before. We couldn't understand how music
could come out of a box.

But, our attention was drawn away from the music when we
saw the small bags waiting for us. We were all very excited as
we opened those bags and discovered an orange, an apple, several pieces of candy and a few different kinds of nuts. This was
a treat worth waiting for. We thought this was a great Christmas.

There was no expectation of receiving a toy, because we
knew that was out of the question. Money was scarce making
it impossible to buy anything other than absolute necessities.
So, there were never any toys bought. The only toys we ever
had were those we could make ourselves. The only exception
was the small wagon I mentioned that dad had bought for us.
There was just no money for extras.

Dad came into the room, saw how happy we were and said, *"Look what that Santa Claus has done — torn out a stone from my chimney!"* Later, we found out that dad had placed that stone there the night before and was playing one of his tricks on us. He, then, got his bag and looked inside, saying, *"Santa didn't give me an orange or an apple, and there is no candy. But, he has left me a few nuts."* He began to crack the nuts one by one, and they were all black and dried up on the inside (another trick from dad). Dad raised his voice and said, *"That Santa has given me nothing but rotten nuts, and he has torn that stone out of my fireplace chimney! Just wait until next Christmas... I will be sitting here with my shotgun. There's no way he is going to get away with this."*

We worried all through the next year wondering what would happen to Santa Claus. Would there be no more paper pokes (bags) in the future? We had no way of knowing what next Christmas would be like.

It is hard to understand how things were back then without being there. At age seven, I didn't know we were poor. It seemed we had just as much as everyone else. In fact, we had everything, but money. We always had food, but we only had meat occasionally. Simple meals were standard fare in most households. What we did eat were potatoes (lots of them) along with sawmill gravy, hoe-cake (thin bread made of cornmeal) and dried beans. Seasons determined many families' menus.

Days of Yore

It is difficult to communicate the days of yore to this present generation. Please remember that my early days, beginning at the age of six, were during the Great Depression of the late 1920s and 1930s, when most everyone had to sacrifice and get by in the best way possible. Neighbors needed each other and assisted each other in a crisis.

Today, elderly people are heard talking about the "good old days." Let me try to paint you a comprehensible mental picture of those days. To understand, you have to seriously think. The generation of today looks upon my generation as ultra conservative and old fashioned. Anyone knows it is not fair nor wise to pass on a judgmental opinion by only looking at the cover of our book of life without a perusal of the conditions and events back then. Therefore, let me attempt to enlighten the reader about the facts of life in our day of long ago.

Hopefully, as you carefully evaluate this document, you will understand that a more truthful picture of my youth and life experiences growing up could not be painted or presented.

I was born before television was invented. In fact, I was twelve years of age before I saw my first radio. To hear it, you had to put on a set of earphones and only one person at a time could hear its program. This was before penicillin, polio shots, frozen foods, Xerox, contact lenses, microwave ovens and most everything else we now take for granted.

Believe it or not, there were very few telephones in a community, and the few phones in existence were party lines. If you had an emergency call to make, sometimes you had to ask gabbing people to please hang up, so you could place your call. Satellites and cell phones were unheard of. There weren't things like radar — it wasn't needed, because travel for most people was by walking or riding on a horse or in a horse drawn wagon.

If you did not have extra money (most people didn't), you couldn't buy things, because credit cards were unheard of. Laser beams and ball-point pens were also unheard of. Man, in his ingenuity, had not yet invented pantyhose, dishwashers, clothes dryers, electric blankets or air conditioners. There was no such thing as FM radio, tape decks, artificial hearts, word processors, yogurt, pizzas, instant coffee or McDonalds. Boys and girls got married first and then lived together. The term "making out" referred to how you did on your school exam. Having a meaningful relationship meant getting along with your kinfolks. In most every family, there was a father and a mother. And, in my generation, we were dense enough to think a woman needed a husband to have a baby. We were not around before the differences between the sexes were discovered, but we were surely around before the sex change came about. Sundays were set aside for many people to attend church as a family to worship God, to help those in need throughout the community, to visit your family and neighbors or just to relax and rest.

My generation grew up before things such as gay rights. Back in those days the laws of the land were against that type of lifestyle. Computer dating, dual careers and day-care centers were non-existent. Mothers stayed home and took care of their children. There was no unisex clothing. Men wore overalls or pants and women wore dresses. Men kept their hair cut short and women did not cut their hair. In the early thirties when a few young women began to cut their hair, a songwriter composed a song that went like this: *"Why do you bob your hair, girls? It's not the thing to do. Just wear it, always wear it, and to your Lord be true."* There were no body piercings and guys were never seen wearing earrings. I don't ever remember any kid blowing his brains out listening to some great band leader like Tommy Dorsey or Harry James.

Our lives were governed by the Ten Commandments (they were promoted and not forbidden in schools or government buildings), good judgment and common sense. We were taught to know the difference between right and wrong and to take responsibility for our actions. Serving your country was a privilege, and living here in America was a much greater privilege. If you saw anything that was stamped with *"Made in Japan,"* you knew that it was junk! Draft dodgers were people who closed doors and windows when the cool evening breeze started blowing, and timesharing meant time the family spent together—not condominiums.

We had five and ten cent stores where you could buy hundreds of items for five and ten cents. The price of ice-cream cones, phone calls, a ride on a streetcar and coca cola were all a nickel a piece. And, if you did not want to splurge, you could spend your nickel on enough stamps to mail a letter and two postcards. You could buy a new Chevy Coupe automobile for $600 and gasoline for only 11 cents per gallon. In fact, a five-pound bag of flour cost 24 cents, a dozen eggs cost 49 cents, a pound of Bacon cost 40 cents and a half gallon of milk cost 28 cents. A forty-hour work week was unheard of. You worked from sun-up to sun-down for approximately one dollar per day.

In my youthful day, "grass" was mowed, "coke" was a soft drink, "pot" was something your mother cooked in and "rock music" was your grandmother rocking in a rocking chair and singing a lullaby. "Aids" were helpers in the principal's office, a "chip" meant a piece of wood, "hardware" was found in a hardware store and "software" wasn't even a word.

In the current generation, many people don't even know the name of their next–door neighbor, whereas in my generation, people were known throughout the area or community and believed in helping each other when needed. You did not have to lock your doors, and in the summer days, you could leave your windows up for fresh air, because there was no worry that someone would come in and do you harm. **That was the "good old days" part.**

With today's generation that has everything that we didn't have plus much more, they are prone to just take everything for granted as though it had always been there. It is no wonder why this present generation refers to us as old and confused, because there is such a wide generation gap, and I am only 96 (Ninety–Six) years old.

Dad's Temper

In the late spring of 1930, dad borrowed a horse to plough his garden. He gave orders for Lorene and me to watch out for our small dog and not to let it get around the horse. When the dog saw that horse, he made a dash out of Lorene's hands and started nipping at the horse's heels. The horse put an end to that by stepping on the little dog.

Dad's temper began to flare again like it had on other occasions. He stopped the horse and yanked his belt out of his trousers. He said, *"I told you what would happen if you didn't take care of that dog."* Lorene stood there, but I ran and crawled as far under the house as I could get.

Lorene was whipped unmercifully, but when I finally came out from under the house, I escaped a thrashing that time, because by that stage dad's temper had cooled down. He seemed to be sorry that he had whipped Lorene so severely.

The Model T Ford—Symbolic of Simpler Times

Lorene Learning to Drive

When Lorene was nine years old, dad thought it was time for her to start learning how to drive an automobile. He put her behind the wheel, cranked the old T-model Ford and, then, got in beside her. They took off and Lorene did quite well for her first test, but when they got back to the house, she cut the wheels too short and ran into the chimney on the side of the house. Everyone, except Lorene, thought it was funny.

Mysterious Sign in The Sky

In the late fall of 1930, the three musketeers—Lorene, Roy and I—were playing in a field near some woods a short distance from the house on a really sunny day. Suddenly, a very dark shadow came over the area where we were playing, but the sun was still shining brightly. It was a large shadow, but there was nothing that we could see that was causing it. We were frightened and ran home to our mother and told her what we had seen. She did not have an answer as to what could have caused it; therefore, it all remained a mystery. Mother told us that it could have been a sign or a warning.

Joy Turned to Grief

Christmas Eve of 1930 finally arrived, and there was great excitement among the McIntyre children. Dad had gone into a small town to purchase some things for his family and was walking home carrying a rather large box, when he fell alongside the road. A couple of fellows came along in an automobile and found dad lying there. They knew him and got him into their car and drove him home. The men, along with mom, thought dad had caught up with some of the men that he knew and had indulged in alcohol. They assumed he had just passed out from drinking on his way home.

Around four o'clock on Christmas morning, my siblings and I awoke with great excitement, and Lorene asked our mother if we could get up. Mother told Lorene to go wake up our father. Lorene called out to dad several times and then said, *"Mother, daddy won't answer, and he is cold."* Mother jumped out of bed and ran to check on dad. Discovering that dad had passed away during the night, she became hysterical for several minutes before being able to compose herself.

This present house where we lived only had one large bedroom, so we all slept in the same room. Mom told us children that we would have to stay there in that room with dad and watch out for our baby sister, because new roads were being cut in the area, and she feared we would get lost if she sent us for help.

As mom started out for help, she saw a light in a neighbor's yard and called out loudly across the hollow. A dear black man answered. Mom told him that dad had passed away, and he told her he would come right over. She, then, flagged down a vehicle, which happened to be a mailman. He took information from mom to let the people in the town know about dad. He, also, volunteered to send a telegram to dad's parents in North Carolina. Later, when dad was examined, it was discovered that he had died from a heart attack instead of alcohol.

Dad's brother, Arthur, had just purchased a new automobile, so he and his father drove it to South Carolina and transported our family back to North Carolina. On the trip, Uncle Arthur stopped at a certain place and let everyone know that this was a nice rest area if anyone had need of one. I was tired of traveling and said, *"I do!"* I thought it would be a place to relax and didn't realize it was just a toilet stop. The only kind of toilet I was used to was the little building that sat behind our house that we called an "outhouse."

Funeral arrangements were made, and the memorial service for dad took place at Norman Grove Baptist Church in Cleveland County, North Carolina on Sunday, December 28th, 1930. Due to snow and heavy rain, dad was laid to rest the next day in the church cemetery. About the only things I remember clearly at his funeral were the song, *"Shall We Gather at the River,"* the coffin, people crying and the heavy rain that was falling. Later, we thought about the dark cloud that had frightened us and wondered if it was a warning concerning dad's death.

Our Destiny

After the funeral, dad's family gathered at our grandparent's home the next week, because of decisions that had to be made. Our mother was not experienced in any factory work and had to take a job in the city of Newton, North Carolina in a factory at minimum wage. She boarded with one of dad's sisters and her family. There was no way she could support four children.

This caused some of the family to feel that there was no alternative, but to place us in an orphanage. But, our paternal grandmother spoke up and said, *"I will not give my consent for these children to be placed in a strange home — they will live here on the farm with us."* In those days there was no social security, no state welfare, no government subsistence or any other society of assistance.

Life on the Farm

So, all four children lived on the farm until our mother was able to get her own place and take Ellen, my youngest sister, with her. Sometime later, Uncle Lee McIntyre, dad's brother, took Roy to live with him and his wife. Lorene and I remained with our grandparents.

My grandmother was a rather small woman, but she took no foolishness and knew how to use a switch. When she felt there was a need, she would send Roy and me to get her a good switch and then use it on both of us. We would both yell like she was really hurting us and, then, run away out of grandma's sight, laughing. After a little bit, we would end up arguing as to which one of us had received the most licks.

On the farm, we soon discovered that our play days were over, because there was endless work to be done. Our days started as early as four o'clock in the morning in order to take care of all the chores before catching the school bus once we were re-enrolled back in school. We both learned to milk a cow, but Lorene did most of the milking plus house work while I took care of many other things that had to be done on a farm, like feeding the hogs and chickens, pasturing the cows after milking, cutting and bringing in the stove and fireplace wood plus other farm work. Thankfully, there was a very good well on the back porch.

One day our grandparents got into a very heated argument that was frightening. From that moment of time, neither one would speak to the other. This went on for several years! When everyone was seated around the dining table at mealtime or working in the field or wherever, and one of my grandparents wanted to get a message to the other grandparent, they would speak through one of us children instead of addressing each other directly.

27

Grandpa would say, *"Tell the old woman thus and thus,"* with grandma right there in the room. Grandma would say, *"Ask the old man thus and thus,"* with grandpa, also, right there in the room. We children had to repeat the message to the one addressed plus the response. The air was always permeated with a heavy tension, which made a very uncomfortable atmosphere for everyone. Holding grudges were very childish settings performed by both grandparents.

The only sweets that we got was mostly jam, jelly, honey, cake or pie which was great; but, I really liked candy, which we seldom were fortunate enough to get any. One day I discovered in the kitchen cabinet a box of Jack Frost brown sugar. I opened the box and it had formed into little balls. I tried one and it was delicious. I kept going back to that box until all of the sugar was gone.

One day grandma wanted some of the sugar and when she opened the box, she discovered it was empty. She asked my sister, Lorene, if she had taken that sugar, and Lorene said, *"No ma'am!"* She, then, asked me if I had taken it, and I said, *"Yes ma'am!"* She said, *"You go and get me a switch for I am going to use it on you."* I followed her orders, and she kept her word. However, Lorene and I would still get into it at times, which earned me the nickname of Jack Frost that Lorene called me. When I think about some of those things today, they are quite humorous.

Fun and Work

Aunt Jennie Bell, dad's youngest sister, was dating a man by the name of Cullie Miller. One Sunday he arrived to see my aunt and suggested taking Roy and me along to a dairy farm close by to buy us some ice cream. We were thrilled, and he bought us all a pint. It was delicious, but after eating a small amount and wanting to appear proper, my aunt said, *"Cullie, I just can't eat any more."* He said, *"That's quite all right; just toss it out."* I said, *"No, don't throw it away, Aunt Jennie Bell. Let me have it."*

When we got home and Cullie had left, Aunt Jennie Bell went to her mother and told her how I had humiliated her. I think it would have been a terrible sin if she had tossed that delicious ice cream out the car window.

On the farm, the crops were diversified. They consisted of corn, cotton, molasses cane, peanuts, sweet potatoes and wheat. The main crop was cotton. There was also a large variety of vegetables raised in a garden that supplied food for the table in summer, and grandma canned many jars of a variety for the winter. When our crops were what we called "laid-by," meaning that they had grown enough that we did not have to hoe them anymore that season, Lorene and I would each take a ten-quart water bucket and go blackberry picking. Our grandmother would make jelly and jam from them.

I was only eight years of age when I had to work in the field hoeing the crops and gathering them. After picking cotton in the fall of the year, in all probability, this must be where the phrase, *"Oh, my aching back,"* derived from. It took a lot of cotton picking to make a five-hundred-pound bale of cotton after all the seeds were separated at the cotton gin. In fact, it filled a large well–packed wagon. I enjoyed going to the gin, pushing the vacuum over the wagon and watching that cotton being sucked up and carried into the gin. When the seeds were removed from the cotton, the seeds were ground into cotton-seed meal to be fed to the cows. The cows loved it.

When I was ten or eleven years of age, I would climb upon the stable partition and bridle the team of mules. I would put the collars and gears on them, ride them out to the field, hook them to a plough and help my granddad plough the field. At noon time, we would unhook the team from the plough and take them to the barn to feed them. Then, we would proceed to the house to eat dinner. Our meals back then were breakfast, dinner and supper without snack breaks. After dinner, we would take our team back to the field, hook them to the plough and continue ploughing.

One day it was very hot and granddad said, *"Wait a minute!"* He walked just a few steps, and there was a copperhead snake laying in the ploughed furrow where it was cool. He killed the snake. I said, *"Granddad, how did you know that snake was there?"* He said, *"Because I sniffed and the air smelled like cucumber."* That was the first time I had heard that a copperhead snake gave off that kind of odor.

Catching Opossums

Granddad had a hunting dog and a very good black man that was a dear friend of ours, who worked the farm that was adjacent to our farm, also had a hunting dog. These two dogs made a team and really chased animals very well together. I loved to fill my pockets with parched peanuts and go opossum hunting at night with my granddad and this neighbor. The dogs would chase the opossums up a tree, and the hunters would get them down and carry them home in a sack. Opossums are scavengers. They were put in cages, fed for six to eight weeks, killed, dressed, parboiled and then baked in an oven with sweet potatoes. They were very delicious.

On a certain night, we were in the woods hunting when the dogs treed what was thought to be an opossum. Our neighbor, carrying the only lantern we had taken, said he would run on ahead and check it out to see if they had treed an opossum.

When he got to the tree and looked up, he pointed his flashlight into the tree. All of a sudden, a bobcat leaped out and landed at his feet. That man was so frightened that he ran off with the lantern and left us in the dark to feel our way out of the woods with just a flashlight. No one became angry at our neighbor, because we thought it was very funny; however, our neighbor never went hunting again without carrying his rifle!

First to Rise Swiftly

In the latter part of the month of October, granddad and I were cutting green corn and hauling it in a wagon to the barn as feed for the stock. At this particular time, the nights were becoming quite cool. Granddad and I were both in bed (we shared the same bed), and I was almost asleep when, suddenly, I jumped out of bed onto the floor, taking the cover along with me and then jumped up and down. Granddad said, *"Ralph, what in the world is the matter with you?"* I said, *"Grandpa, something was crawling up my leg and was scratching me!"* Lorene lit a lamp and we looked, but nothing could be found. Reluctantly, I crawled back into bed.

The next morning as I was dressing and bent down to pick up my pants, there lay a lizard barely under the bed that had been stomped to death. At the breakfast table, I told the others I had discovered that it was a lizard crawling on me, which caused me to jump out of bed in a panic. My reaction of jumping up and down had actually caused me to stomp the poor lizard to death. Granddad began to laugh and said, *"That lizard was crawling up my leg and I flipped it over on you, and I thought you were going to tear the house down!"*

31

A Different Day Between "Then" And "Now"

In those days the children got one pair of shoes a year. I got mine when the last bale of cotton was sold, which was late October or around the first of November. There were usually frosty mornings before shoes could be bought, and this sure made a person step lively! Before the first of April, those shoes would be worn out. I would put thick cardboard in mine until it got warm enough to go barefoot.

In going barefoot all summer, I often stumped my big toes on stones. Also, one of the cows or mules would step or stomp on them, sometimes, and knock the nails off. This happened so many times that both of these big toenails would grow back a little thicker each time. Finally, they became like a turtle shell for hardness, which I have had to live with ever since.

When I would be permitted to go to Sunday school or any other place in the summertime, I had to go in my bare feet. Church was about a two-mile walk from the farm, and I loved to go every Sunday that was possible. My grandparents were not Christians and neither was I; however, I heard enough Scripture in those Sunday school days to cause me to believe that the Bible was the Word of God. Most of the people that did not even attend church in those days were God-minded.

One Sunday I was going to church, and the sun was very bright. There was a boy in my grade school that lived nearby. I looked up the road and saw a red glow coming from the roof of his house. I thought, *"That doesn't look like the light of the sun."* I began to run toward his house, and when I got closer, I realized his roof was on fire. I ran as fast as I could. I yelled out to a man in the yard and told him the roof was on fire. The man grabbed a ladder and was able to get water and extinguish the fire.

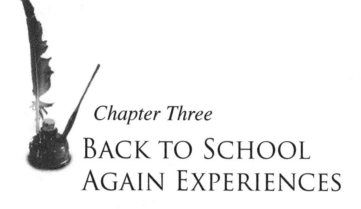

Chapter Three

BACK TO SCHOOL AGAIN EXPERIENCES

In January of 1931, Lorene and I were enrolled in school at Startown, North Carolina, which consisted of all eleven grades. The twelfth grade in American schools had not been instituted into the school system at this time. Since we had missed half of the school year, I was not able to grasp enough of the material to pass to the next grade and had to repeat the second grade. Lorene, being older, breezed through and progressed to the third grade.

Some children had parents that did very well financially, and they had nice book bags, lunch boxes and had sandwiches made with store-bought bread (what we call loaf bread or light bread today). However, these children were definitely in the minority.

On the farm, money was rather hard to come by, and Lorene and I had to carry our lunch of cornbread and side pork meat in a paper poke (bag). We never ate lunch together, but we both would go somewhere by ourselves to eat, because we felt there were others that would make fun of what we had to eat. I suppose this was youthful pride, because there were many other students in the same boat. These were the days of the Great Depression, and people (in general) did not even recognize the poverty they lived in, because most everyone was there themselves.

Enough is Enough

Lorene was old enough to take care of herself and other students left her alone, but some of the boys were always picking on me. On the school bus going home, there was one boy by the name of Clyde Huffman, who would pick on me almost every day. One time, I kept taking his harassment until tears started running down my face. Then, the other boys and girls began laughing at me. I balled up my fist and hit Clyde in the left eye, knocking him off his seat.

Then, someone grabbed me from behind. Without looking, I whirled around and hit that person, too. Little did I realize that I was hitting one of the teachers by the name of Lois Bost. I figured I would now have to report to the principal's office to be punished the next day. But, upon reflection, I decided that regardless of the outcome, I had no regrets for my actions except for hitting the teacher, because I really liked her.

My grandparents had informed me that if I got into fights or was punished at school, when I got home, I would get another switching. They, also, told Lorene that if she did not report to them any time that I got into trouble, then she would be punished, too.

When we got home and Lorene gave her report, my granddad went outside and cut two rather strong switches. However, to my surprise, he handed them to me instead of switching me. Granddad instructed me to take those switches with me the next day, give them to the school bus driver and tell him that he had permission to use them any time in the future that I got into another fight.

I gave the switches to the bus driver and told him what my granddad had said. He just grinned and tossed them aside. I think he was even happy that I had hit Clyde. Also, I had to tell Miss Bost that I was sorry that I had hit her. I had become so angry at Clyde that I had become blind.

I would have preferred that my granddad had used those switches on me instead of me having to carry out his orders. But, truthfully, I felt a little better when I looked at Clyde and saw his very black eye. The good part was what happened between Clyde and me after this incident. The next time he saw me, he looked at me and grinned. In fact, none of those boys ever picked on me again. We all became long-lasting friends. The other good news about this incident was the fact that Miss Bost did not report this matter to the principal.

Roy Takes a Nose Dive

The school bus driver would let Roy open the door at our stop every day. One time, he yanked the door open before the bus had stopped and kept going right out the door, landing on the edge of the road. The driver stopped and jumped off the bus, but Roy got up off the ground laughing. It was no laughing matter when we got home, though, because he got a good switching. The next day he had to take a switch and give it to the driver to use if he attempted to open that door again while the bus was still moving.

At school, the paddle was used to keep proper order in those days. The classroom doors were usually left open to the hall in warm weather. One day someone down the hall from my class room was heard getting a heavy paddling. Several of the students looked at me and said, *"I bet that is your brother."* That didn't set too well with me. At lunchtime, I said to Roy, *"Boy, someone was really getting a paddling this morning."* Roy just grinned. I said, *"That was you?"* He said, *"It didn't hurt."*

Studying by Fire Light

There was no such thing as being able to remain after school and participate in any sports. We had to catch the bus and come straight home from school; however, we could not get the homework done while it was daylight, because there was daily work on the farm that lasted all the way until darkness set in.

Since there was no electricity on the farm, the source of light was kerosene lamps and lanterns. Lorene and I had to lay on our stomach and study our school homework by the light from the fireplace, because our grandparents would not let us waste the oil in the lamps. I was able to pass on my school homework, but Lorene, even under those conditions, excelled and became the Valedictorian of her graduating class.

Lorene Graduates as Valedictorian 1940

36

A big thing that we enjoyed at school in those days, especially during recess and lunch times, were marble games. Lorene was ahead of me in academics and book learning, but I was way ahead of her in playing marble games. She and my peers knew that I was difficult to beat. Sometimes, I would be in trouble when I got home, because the knees of my pants would be very dirty from shooting those marbles.

Business Endeavor

One of my schoolmates owned the paper route for the *Charlotte Observer* newspaper in Claremont. The route consisted of about three hundred customers. When he developed heart problems, he offered to let me have the route if I would buy his nearly new bicycle for thirty-five dollars. He was willing to let me pay weekly out of my weekly commission.

With my grandparents' permission, I took the route over with the understanding that I would have to keep up with my responsibilities on the farm. This new endeavor added about two-and-one-half hours to the chores I already had; therefore, I had to arise each morning around four o'clock to get it all completed.

Occasionally, for different reasons, the papers would arrive late. I had to wait until they arrived and then deliver them. One morning they were late and caused me to be two hours late arriving for my classes at school.

There was one customer on my route by the name of Claud Miller who owned a filling (gasoline) station and grocery store. His place was close to the end of my paper route. When I arrived at his place, he said, *"Where have you been?"* I said, *"My papers were late in arriving."* He said, *"When those papers are late you deliver mine first."* I said, *"My other customers want their papers just the same as you, and I am already two hours late for school.*" He walked over and slapped me hard on the side of my face. Right at that moment, I wanted to go home, get my granddad's shotgun that he let me use at times, bring it back and shoot this man. I am glad when I cooled down that I lost that desire.

My granddad always cautioned me to be very careful when using his twelve-gauge double-barrel shotgun. His advice came from a wisdom of experience. Once when he went squirrel hunting, he spotted a squirrel in a tall tree. He raised his shot gun and fired it. However, something happened that had never happened before. He thought he had pulled only one trigger, but both barrels fired at once. The kickback from that gun was so powerful that it knocked my granddad off his feet. The gun flew out of his hands and went sailing over his head. It nose–dived with both barrels stuck deep in the soft ground from recent rain. Granddad was able to get up and began looking for his black brimmed hat. The ground was sloped and his hat had rolled all the way down the slope. His shoulder was badly bruised, but he was very thankful that the shoulder was not broken. From his experience, I always put a shell in only one barrel for my safety sake.

Arriving late at school due to the late delivery of my papers, the principal saw me and instructed me to report to my home room teacher to let her know that I would make up the time after the school day was over. He did this, although he knew that this would get me in trouble at home. So, I headed for my next class since it was time to change classes. All of a sudden, someone hit me in the back very hard. Whirling around, I was face to face with the principal. He said, *"I told you to report to your home room teacher."* I said, *"I thought you meant for me to inform her in my next home room class."* He said, *"When*

I give you orders to do something, I mean now." I never liked that man after that. I thought he was very unreasonable.

Between the farm work, the school work and the paper route work, I was exhausted when the day came to an end. When bedtime came around, there was no argument about having to turn in early. Our bed mattresses were known as straw ticks. Straw was taken from thrashed wheat and used to fill what was called a tick, which was the size of a regular mattress. It was really a very good and comfortable bed that had that fresh farm aroma. After my very long days, it was so refreshing to finally crawl upon that mattress and go to sleep.

Ralph Age 16 – Lorene Age 18

Chapter Four
NEW ADVENTURE

W e had to pack up and move, because granddad leased another farm that was, somewhat, larger than what we had from a Mr. Coulter. It was truly a nice farm with a great well for water, but there was no inside plumbing or electricity. There was a team of mules and a horse that was needed for working this farm.

When Lorene and I would get all of the work on our farm caught up, we would work for other farmers for pay. We were paid ten cents an hour to work in a field or one cent a pound to pick cotton. Also, in the spring, we picked strawberries for eight cents a gallon. We were thrilled that we could make a little money for ourselves. This doesn't sound very exciting today, but back then, you could buy a loaf of bread for five cents. However, there were problems with this, because there were times when a farmer never paid us after we had done the work agreed upon.

My experience on the farm was worth its weight in gold, although I didn't realize this at the time. I cherish those days now very much. It would be a great benefit to anyone to have the opportunity to spend time on a farm. It takes patience, because everything that is done takes a great deal of time:

plowing and preparing the ground, planting the different seeds for the variety of products, cultivating and hoeing the crops to get rid of the weeds and watching them mature into their fullness to be harvested.

Our cousins, Bryon Coonie (B.C.), Frances, Mary Ella, Bill and Geraldine Sweezy, would visit the farm from the city of Newton, North Carolina, which was always refreshing and enjoyable. It was always a thrill to be in their company, and they were also very happy to be in our company, too. We were all in the same age range and, therefore, we had much fun together.

On one particular day, B.C. had mounted the mule and then stuck out his foot for a stirrup for me to get on behind him. But, the mule thought differently. Suddenly, he kicked me in the stomach so hard that I landed about eight feet from him in a briar patch. I had to lie there for a while until the pain subsided, and I got my breath back. Lying in that briar patch all scratched up was a very comical sight. B.C. almost fell off the mule laughing while I desired to kill that mule. I don't know whether something rubbed the leg of the mule or not, because he had always been very gentle. But, there was something that spooked him and caused him to react like he did that remains a mystery to this very day.

On another memorable day when B.C. came to visit, we were having a lot of fun when B.C. and I entered a storage building with a loft. B.C. saw a movement under a cover in the loft and said, *"There are mice under that covering. You go up in the loft, raise that cover and I will grab them."* When I climbed up into the loft, B.C. was standing on the ladder half way up into the loft ready to grab the mice. When I reached out and lifted the cover, B.C. yelled, *"Snake"* and fell through the loft opening. I had nowhere to escape while a very large black snake, approximately six feet in length, came slithering out from under that cover. It almost passed over my feet on its way out of a window and onto the ground.

Every year during the week of the fourth of July there was a gathering in Newton, North Carolina for an event called *"Old Soldiers Reunion."* People looked forward to this every year. It was similar to the carnivals of today except they were more family oriented. Thursday was youth day and for fifty-cents, we could ride all of their rides. There were sack-races, greasy-pig races, climbing a greasy pole plus other entertainment. It was five miles from our house to Newton, but we always hooked the mule team to our wagon and rode to this city for this gathering.

Field of Cotton Ready for Picking

During cotton picking time when the fields were white, there were times when some of the farmers did not have enough help to get all of their cotton picked. In those days, all of the cotton picking had to be done by hand. So, the community would come together and have what was known as *"A Neighbor Cotton Picking Day."*

A certain day, (usually a Saturday), would be planned where those from neighboring farms would join together and help their neighbor. In the evening after the day's work was finished, everyone enjoyed a great meal together that the ladies had spent time cooking. After the meal, musicians with string instruments would begin playing music, and some of the folks would enjoy a good time of dancing. This is probably the only time that I enjoyed picking cotton.

Neighborhood Corn Shucking

Another time that was quite enjoyable was called a "corn-shucking." One of the farmers would gather all of his corn from the fields and pile it in long piles about six feet wide and four feet high. The length of the piles varied according to the amount of corn gathered. The shucking usually took place in the evening time when other farmers had their work finished for the day.

When they had this event, some of the farmers would hide a half gallon to a gallon of whiskey in the row of corn, and most of those gathered hoped they would be the one to find it. When whosoever did find it, they always shared it with all that wanted to have a drink or two. The speed of shucking the corn by some that had gathered for that purpose was amazing. Before you realized it, all of the corn was shucked, and everyone had headed to the house for another great meal and more music and dancing.

Farm Work Never Ends

Livestock on a farm has to be cared for regardless of the day, season or weather. Much of this chore fell to my lot. If there was a creek or stream close by, the horses and mules were bridled and taken there for water. If not, water had to be drawn by bucket from the well. After milking, the cows were turned into a pasture where there was water.

The exception to this was winter storms, which caused me to have to carry water to the barn for them. Through the cold of winter, fresh straw was put in the stables, periodically, instead of cleaning out the waste. When springtime arrived, these stables certainly needed a lot of shoveling and cleaning out. Again, I was on the job taking care of this chore. My shoes were worn out by this time of the year, and I had to stand in that manure half-way up to my knees barefooted and pitch that waste into a wagon. We, then, would haul it to the field and spread it over the farmland, because it made great fertilizer.

Between Two Points

One day I will never forget was when Roy came to granddad's place for a few days' visit. The cows got out of the pasture, and we decided to guide them back to the barn. However, this one cow had a strong mind of her own and took off running. Then, the chase was on. I was able to outrun her, but when I got alongside of her, she slung her head and caught her horns in the back of my overalls. When she threw her head back, I was on top of her head between her pointed horns and couldn't get loose. This scared cow with me riding on her horns headed for a brush thicket; but, Roy was running fast and was able to catch her by the tail. He swung her hard which spun her around. This caused me to be slung off her horns and, fortunately, landed me in a soft pile of sand. After everything settled down, we started thinking how funny this episode was and could hardly stop laughing. Nevertheless, we were very glad that there was no one around with a camera.

In Preparation

Thankfully, there was plenty of trees on the farm since wood was used for the cooking stove and fireplaces. This meant that the wood boxes in the house had to be restocked every evening. When you happen to be the one that must rise from a nice warm bed around four or five o'clock in the morning to build the fires, you learn very soon how to get a good fire burning quickly.

I would go to the woods and find old pine stumps that were decaying. I looked for the part called the *"heart,"* because the "heart" would be solid and very rich with resin that burned easily and quickly. This solved the concern about the fire dying out. When we could not do any kind of work on the farm in the wintertime due to snow, we went into the woods and cut down trees into the proper length and size for house use.

Many bushels of sweet potatoes were produced on the farm. One day when I was walking through the potato field with their vines covering all of the ground, I stepped on a fruit jar that had been broken. The bottom of my foot was cut all the way to the bone. It was bleeding profusely. My grandmother took soot from the fireplace and packed the wound full to stop the bleeding. Home remedies were the order of the day, because doctors were never considered unless it was a near death situation. While it healed, I hobbled around on my heel and continued taking care of my share of the home chores plus going to school every day.

Chapter Five
MOVING YET AGAIN

My grandfather leased another farm, because the present one was being sold. It was a place called Bunker Hill, which was a rather remote place. One of the roads leading to the farm had a covered bridge over a creek called *"Lyle Creek."* The state of North Carolina made this a historic state park after we had lived there.

Covered Bridge Crossing Lyle Creek – Claremont, NC
(Presently a State Park)

Some of the family thought this farm was a terrible place, but I loved it. The house dated back to pre-Civil War days, and it was another place without electricity or inside plumbing; however, thankfully, there was a good well at the back of the house. This farm had been the property of a plantation owner during the Civil War. Some of the floors of the house had dull reddish stains of what was said to be the blood of some disobedient slaves that had been beaten by their master. My bedroom floor was one of these blood-stained floors.

One area close to the house was a swamp that was full of bull frogs, which could be heard croaking during the night. This suited me just fine. I loved to hear them croaking. Lyle Creek was a good place for fishing and, also, had some good swimming holes. This place was ideal for hunting, because there was a variety of animals.

I made several rabbit boxes to trap rabbits. I would bait the traps with apples or something else that would draw their attention. I caught many rabbits in a very humane way without any suffering involved whatsoever. These rabbits provided much food. What our family could not eat, I was able to sell to a grocer. He paid me twenty-five cents for each rabbit that I had cleaned and dressed. I had to leave the hind feet on, so the grocer could make sure that it was truly a rabbit. Although hunting in the woods was a lot of fun, there was one thing you had to watch out for – the danger of copperhead snakes.

At this farm, Lorene and I had to switch schools to the city of Catawba, North Carolina. To catch the school bus, we had to walk approximately three quarters of a mile on a dirt or mud road, depending on the weather, to catch the school bus. We both fit in with the other students quite well.

I was in the sixth grade at this time, and I became friends with a very nice-looking girl. Once in a while on a Saturday, this twelve-year-old boy would sweet talk his grandmother into letting him go visit with her, which was a distance of two miles.

Of course, I had to be home in time to do the evening chores. There is nothing like falling in love at age twelve, but to my dismay, she married another boy when she was only sixteen years of age.

Visiting Another Cousin

One summer I was given permission to spend a week with my Uncle Arthur in Statesville, North Carolina, who had a son my age by the name of Victor. We had a great time, and Uncle Arthur asked if we would like to go turtle hunting with him, which we readily agreed. We went to the creek, and Uncle Arthur took a stout stick and probed along the banks of the creek just underwater. When he struck something solid, he could tell immediately if it was a stone or a turtle. If it was a turtle, he would reach his hand under the water into that bank and pull the turtle out by its tail.

I volunteered to carry the sack, which had five rather large turtles. As I was kind of dragging the sack along, Uncle Arthur said, *"Ralph, put the sack over your shoulder and carry them."* I replied, *"Uncle Arthur, I'm afraid they will bite me."* Uncle Arthur said, *"They won't bite through that sack. Put that sack over your shoulder."* I put the sack over my shoulder, crawled out of the creek and started across a meadow.

Suddenly, I let out a loud yelp and threw the sack of turtles, fanning all five of them into the meadow. After chasing and catching all five turtles and putting them back into the sack, Uncle Arthur scolded me for throwing the sack like that. I said, *"Uncle Arthur, one of those turtles bit me through that sack and my pants."* He did not believe me until I pulled my pants down, and he saw that my leg was already turning black. Uncle Arthur apologized and said, *"I would have thrown that sack myself!"*

No Dull Moments on A Farm

There was a mare on the farm that gave birth to a beautiful colt. I took over the responsibility of caring for him. We had a lot of fun playing together. He grew rapidly, and I wanted to mount him and take a ride. A very fine black neighbor that we called "Uncle Ed" said, *"Ralph, I will hold the bridle and give you a hand to get aboard, if you are sure you want to ride him."*

As soon as I settled onto his back, all four of that young colt's feet left the ground. If it had not been for the kind neighbor grabbing my arm and lifting me off, I would have gone sailing through the air. I decided then and there that I did not any longer want to ride him.

There was a variety of fowl raised on the farm including chickens, turkeys, guineas and ducks. There was no trouble in finding the chicken or duck nests, but it was a very different story trying to find the turkey and guinea nests. They were very cagy, and they would lead off opposite to where they had their nest until they felt they were not being observed. Then, they would change course and zigzag their way back to their nest.

It took patience, but I would find a good place for observation and watch them continuously until I spotted their secret place. One time when I had been to the nest and was coming back through a thick patch of vines, my bare foot stepped on something quite cold, and I immediately knew it was a snake. Jumping as far as I could, I, then, looked back and spotted a black snake about five or six feet in length slithering off through the vines.

Humbled Again

Granddad always made a long sweet potato slip (plant) bed. After a rain, neighbors from all around came to purchase those slips, because this was the best time for setting them in the ground. This saved time and energy by not having to haul barrels of water when they were set in the ground. Granddad not only sold slips to other farmers, but set out a large field of slips on our farm, also.

When potato digging time arrived, they had to be ploughed out of the ground and separated from their vines. These were assorted and placed in crates. The purchaser would drive through the field to load them on his truck.

I was about twelve years of age, and I daydreamed at times instead of working. On such a day, we were all working in the potato field close to the time for the truck to arrive. This was a time that I, down on my knees, chose to let my mind wander instead of boxing potatoes—that is until, suddenly, I landed on my face in the dirt from a swift kick in my behind from my granddad, who said, *"Ralph, I don't want to see you daydreaming again. Start packing those potatoes."* If he had known what I was daydreaming about, he would probably have kicked me again. My dream was of the day when I would be able to get off of this farm.

Many times in the summer on those very warm nights I would lay flat on my back in the grass, look up at the sky filled with glittering stars, ponder and wonder if there was anything more in life than what I was experiencing. The view was beautiful and, once in a while, I would see what was called a shooting star streak across the sky.

Work on a farm from day to day is a continuing cycle or repetition. Today, I have the deepest respect for our farmers that follow this pattern to supply us our different foods. Everyone should bow their heads at meal time and be thankful that God has put into the hearts of certain people to work the farms. But, most people just take them for granted. The jobs of farmers are very essential and honorable.

Chapter Six

NEW MOVE OFF THE FARM FOR GOOD

G randdad contracted for another farm owned by a man named Pink Wilson, which was about four miles from Bunker Hill. Everything had to be moved on a wagon pulled by a team of horses. This was a slow process that took a couple of days to complete. This was the fourth farm we had lived on since we had come to live with our grandparents, but it was the best place of them all and located approximately one mile outside of Claremont, North Carolina. Lorene and I had to transfer from the Catawba school to the Claremont school. The walk to catch the school bus was shorter, and the road did not get muddy when it rained.

One day it was rather cool outside, so granddad and I were sitting by the fireplace where a good fire was burning. Granddad chewed tobacco, and he pulled his pocket knife out and proceeded to cut him off a plug of tobacco to put in his mouth. He started to replace the tobacco and knife in his pocket, when he looked at me and said, *"Ralph would you like to have a chew of tobacco?"* I was shocked. I looked at grandpa and said, *"Yessir!"* He cut me off a plug and I put it in my mouth and began to chew on it. I was feeling grownup. It wasn't long until I began to feel kind of sick. I got up from my chair and started to leave the room, when granddad said, *"Ralph, where are you going?"* I said, *"I think I will go outside for a while."* Granddad said, *"No, it's cold outside. Sit back down."* I sat down, but it wasn't long until I jumped up and left the room before he could stop me again. I was sick. I never wanted another chew of tobacco.

Granddad and another farmer decided they would supplement their finances by setting up a "still" and making a run of illegal whiskey (white lightening). I spent my free time in the woods with my rifle, and I could move about noiselessly like an American Indian. Not knowing about my granddad's venture, I came upon them by accident. I carelessly stepped on a stick and it snapped, which really got their attention. So, I stood motionless behind a tree until they relaxed and went back to their work. Easing myself backward, I was able to leave them behind without being seen. I told my grandmother about their endeavor. She wanted me to report it to the sheriff, but I told her that I couldn't do that.

I worked for other farmers as often as was possible, which permitted me to save five dollars. I wanted a bicycle in the worst kind of way, and I knew a boy that had one for sale. So, I bought it with my five dollars. The pedals were broken off and two bolts were used for pedals. The wheels were warped, too, but my uncle Otis came in on leave from the U. S. Army and helped me fix the bicycle. He adjusted the spokes, aligned the wheels and made them much better. I got much enjoyment from that worn out bicycle.

Foxy Chicken Thieves

I became friends with a couple of brothers by the last name of Hewitt. Their dad owned a grocery store in Claremont. Once in a while, Roy and I would catch one of our grandmother's chickens, place a string around its leg and tie it to a tree. We would, then, proceed to beg our grandmother to let us go to the store for something she needed. On our way, we would cut through the woods to pick up our prisoner chicken and go to town. One of us would hold the chicken, and the other one would go into the store and get one of the Hewitt boys to come out back to get the chicken and pay us for it. In doing it this way, their dad did not know where the chicken had come from. Above all, we didn't want him mentioning this episode to our granddad. Grandma knew every chicken she had, and she accused foxes of catching her chickens. We felt as though we worked on the farm hard enough to at least deserve a chicken now and then.

There was a large field on the farm planted in peanuts, which was ploughed out of the ground and stacked to dry or cure. Then, we would haul them to a vacant house on the farm and pile them into a large room. On rainy days, Lorene and I had to go there and pull the peanuts off the vines. It was a monotonous job for sure. One day, while pulling the peanuts off the vines, I ate too many of those raw nuts and got so sick. I had to go home and go to bed. I was sick for a couple of days.

Tenants by the name of Wesson worked the farm next to our farm. They had a son by the name of Roy, who was a high school teacher. Roy would come to spend the summers with his parents. He and I became good friends. Roy would come over to our farm often, and we made some slingshots. We would

55

practice shooting with them until we became very good. In fact, we got to where we hardly ever missed our target.

We had a huge barn where the rats had built themselves a den in one side of the barn. Roy and I cut us a long pole, and one of us would poke that pole into the den until a rat would run out across the overhead beam. While one of us was poking with the pole, the other one was standing by for the rat to run across the beam, so we could knock it off with a shot from our slingshot.

I had a small fox terrier dog that loved this. As soon as that rat hit the ground, he would snatch it up and sling it from side to side until it was dead. Then, he would lay it aside and wait for another one to be knocked off the beam. We got rid of quite a few rats that way. We also had a king snake and a black snake that stayed in the barn, and they caught quite a few rats, too.

Some Things are Worth the Penalty

Going to the school bus stop one morning, about one-quarter of a mile from our house, I asked Lorene if she would take care of my books. She said, *"You can take care of your own books."* I said, *"I am not going to school. I am going to see our mother."* Lorene said, *"She lives in Hickory and that is eight miles away. How are you going to get there? Also, you will be in bad trouble!"* I said, *"I am going to walk and see mother even if I do get into trouble."*

So, she kept my books, and I started out walking. I had walked less than half the distance, when an automobile stopped. A very nice man gave me a ride the rest of the way. I certainly enjoyed my day, but my mother persuaded me to return to the farm that evening and paid my fare on the train.

When I arrived home about six o'clock in the evening, granddad called out and said, *"Ralph I need you over here."* My granddad had cut two very strong switches (sticks) that were about one-quarter of an inch in diameter at the small end. He said, *"I am going to give you a whipping."* But, he did not give me a whipping—he gave me an unmerciful beating. He wore those sticks out on me. He kept beating me, because I would not cry. He said, *"I am going to whip you until you cry."* I settled it in my mind not to give him the satisfaction of crying. I refused to cry even if this beating killed me. I wanted to fall on my knees and let the tears flow, but I was determined not to give my granddad that pleasure he so desired.

After a little while, grandma came out and yelled, *"Stop beating him! That's enough!"* I always highly respected my grandfather, but at that time, I truly hated him. The next day I told Lorene that my back was raw and still stinging, and that I had not been able to sleep all night, because of the pain. During school for several days, I had to sit straight up at my desk to keep the pressure off of my back.

That was the first time and the last time granddad ever beat me, and grandma never whipped me again either. I have never been one to hold a grudge. When my back healed, I began to think back about everything my grandparents had done for the benefit of us children. They sacrificed much by taking us into their home to live with them, which spared us from being placed into an orphanage to live among strange people. Deep in my heart, I completely forgave my grandfather. I truly loved and respected him.

Mixed Emotions

Lorene and I worked very hard on the farm. In fact, in the fall of the year, we did most of the hoeing during the growth season and the picking of the cotton crop during the harvest season.

One day granddad didn't like the way I had done a certain thing and got on my case very hard. He said, *"Remember what I gave you awhile back, I can do it all over again."* I said, *"Yes sir, Grandpa, I remember; but, don't you ever try that again."* He looked at me for several seconds. I just stared him down. Finally, he turned and walked away. Nothing more was ever said.

Moving On

Ever since the beating I received from my granddad, things were never the same between us. There was a cold feeling, which put a distance between us. After some time and much thought, I realized it was time for me to depart from the farm. Checking around, I found a boy that would pay my asking price for the paper route including my bicycle.

The night before my departure I packed a few things in a small suitcase and hid it under the porch steps. Leaving my grandparents, who thought I had gone to deliver papers, I picked up my suitcase and knew that I was leaving for good. I was happy that I was leaving, but on the other hand, I felt bad to be leaving my sister, Lorene, without explaining things to her. We had always been very close. I caught an early train and rode about fifty miles. From there, I planned to hitchhike.

I had the highest respect for soldiers. I met up with one on my trip who wound up conning me out of what little money

I had. With no more money, I had no other choice except to depend on catching a ride by hitch hiking. I had no idea where I was going. I just started sticking out my thumb to hitch a ride. I met a man that was also hitchhiking. He asked me, *"Have you had anything to eat, today?"* I said, *"No."* He went into a grocery store and came back a short time later. The grocer had given him some cheese and crackers, which he shared with me. He suggested that we should hang out at this gasoline station in hopes of catching a ride.

A tractor and trailer driver pulled in, and he was able to get a ride with this driver. However, due to my young age, the driver would not take me aboard, because he was going to cross a state line. Again, I was left on my own. Then, I located the road that would take me to Charlotte, North Carolina. I walked out of the town of Salisbury and started hitchhiking.

After taking a rest by sitting on my suitcase, I stood up to try to catch a ride. But, when I saw this car approaching, I soon recognized it to be a state patrolman. I turned my back on him thinking he would zoom on past me, which he did. But, instead of continuing on, he came to a stop and began backing up. I wanted to run, but knew that I would really be in trouble if I did. It was not my nature to lie, but I knew that I had better think of things to tell him that would be convincing.

When he backed up to where I was, he asked me, *"Where are you going?"* I informed him that I was going to Charlotte. He told me to get in the car. When I did, he drove off very fast and continued at a high rate of speed. He asked me many questions, and I gave him ready answers, although they were not true. We passed the "Jackson Training School for Boys." He pointed it out and informed me that was the home of wayward boys. He asked me what my age was, and I told him that I was fourteen years of age. He then asked me, *"Why are you going* to Charlotte?" I replied, "My aunt lives there and is down very sick. She wants me to come and be with her for a few days, because she has no one else to help her."

I was convincing, and he accepted my answer. He informed me that he was on an emergency call or else he would have taken me to my aunt's address. I relaxed, but that part was true — it really was my aunt's address. He dropped me off, gave me good directions and wished me good luck.

Feelings of Anxiety

I tried my luck at hitchhiking again, but no one would pick me up. It was getting late in the afternoon, and I had this strong feeling that I should let my mother know my plans so she would not be worried. My mother was a very good woman, and she had to work very hard. I began to walk back through town for several miles before I started hitchhiking again.

Finally, a man stopped and gave me a lift to Mount Holly, North Carolina. By this time, it was dark. I went into a small grocery store and talked to the owner for a little while. I informed him that it was hard to catch a ride. He was a good judge of character, because he gave me, who was very hungry, a pack of cinnamon raisin buns that were very filling. I was most grateful for his act of kindness. Then, he said, *"It is not likely that you will be able to catch a ride this late in the day. Why don't you go across the street to the police station and ask them if they have an empty cell where you can spend the night?"*

By this time, I was getting a little desperate, so across the street I went. When I walked into the station, an officer about six feet in height and weighing approximately two hundred pounds asked in a gruff voice, *"What can I do for you?"* Using the same lie I had told the state patrolman, I said, *"Officer, I have been in Charlotte with a sick aunt and am now heading to my home in Hickory. It has begun to rain. Would you have an extra bed that I could sleep on tonight?"* He just looked at me for a while, and I became nervous. Then, he said, *"Son, you are in luck as things are a little slow tonight. We do have an extra bed."* He led me back to a cell, gave me bed covers and asked, *"Would you like for me to lock the bars?"* I said, *"No Sir!"* He laughed and went back to his office. I felt quite safe and did get a good night's rest.

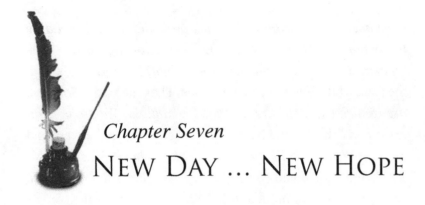

Chapter Seven

NEW DAY ... NEW HOPE

Awaking quite early the next morning, I came out of my cell and approached the officer on duty. After expressing my appreciation for his kindness and generosity, I crossed the street and went into the grocery store again. Thanking the grocer for his great help, I was headed for the door when he stopped me. I turned around, and he handed me another nice pack of cinnamon raisin buns. It was one of the best meals I ever ate and definitely a most needed one.

The rain had stopped, and I felt good about my decision to return to Hickory to let my mother know my plans. I had not been hitchhiking very long, when a real nice gentleman stopped and gave me a lift. He asked, *"Where are you heading to?"* I thanked him for stopping and picking me up, and said, *"I am on my way to my mother's house in Hickory."* He said, *"Great! I can give you a lift to Conover, which will be approximately five miles from your destination."*

Arming myself with some more falsehoods as I figured I was in for some heavy grilling; I was surprised because that didn't happen. I sat back and began to enjoy my ride. When we came into the city limits of Lincolnton, North Carolina, this kind man said, *"I need to stop here for a short period."* I replied, *"That will be fine with me as I am thankful for the ride."* Shortly, he pulled in and parked in front of a restaurant. Looking at me, he said, *"Let us go in and get a sandwich and a cup of coffee."* I said, *"Thanks! Go right ahead, but if you don't mind, I will just sit here and wait for you."* He said, *"It's damp and cool out here—just come on in and sit with me while I eat."*

We went inside. When the waitress took his order, I thought that he must really be hungry, because he ordered a double order of everything. When the waitress brought the order, he told her to sit half of the order in front of me and said, *"This looks good! Let's eat!"* I didn't say a word, but I had to restrain myself to keep from just wolfing that wonderful food down without chewing.

After our meal, we were back in the car and on the road again. It was easy to talk to this man. I discovered that he was a salesman for a large company and had to travel quite a bit. When we arrived in Conover, he made a turn and headed toward Hickory instead of letting me out of his automobile and taking his planned route. I said, *"Your route went straight back at the light!"* He said, *"It is only five miles more for you, and I have a little extra time so I will run you on home."*

He had treated me so kind that I almost burst into tears, but trying to be grown up, I fought them back. It wasn't long until he was dropping me off in front of my mother's house. After I thanked him graciously, he drove away. I never saw that man again, but I never forgot him.

With Gladness and Apprehension

No one was home when I arrived. My mother was at work in a full fashion hosiery mill. My brother, who was now living with our mother along with my youngest sister, were both in school. My brother was extremely thrilled when he came home and found me sitting on the front porch. When mother arrived home, she was glad to see me, but I could see the strain of wonderment on her face.

I said, *"Mother, I haven't come here to make things harder for you, but I came to let you know that I have left the farm for good. Now, don't worry! I am fourteen years of age. I have always been large for my age,* and I *know how to work. So, I will be on my way, and I will make it on my own. If I don't, I will go to the Jackson Training School for delinquent boys before I will return to the farm, because granddad has become very unreasonable."* Mother said, *"Let us go in and prepare a meal, and we will talk about it."*

When dinner was finished and everything was put away, we all gathered in the living room and began to discuss what would be best for every one of us. I was determined to strike out on my own, but my brother and sister—especially my brother— begged me to stay there with them. I told them that in all fairness to mom, it was best that I leave. Finally, mother said, *"You stay here and let us try things for a while to see if we can, somehow, make it all work; but, in the meantime, I want you back in school."* My brother, Roy, let out a big loud whoop. The next day I was enrolled in Hickory High School.

Back in Business

Roy had a paper route, and he asked those in charge if there was an opening for another delivery boy, because his brother had come there to live. They told him to have me to come in the next morning. They were happy to let me have a route that had come open, but I would have to have a bicycle, because this route covered quite a large area.

Roy and I went to a Firestone store and looked at bicycles they had for sale. I found one that I really liked, but the price was thirty-five dollars. I explained to the salesman that I was just hired for a paper route, but I would have to have a bicycle to do the job. I asked him if there was some way I could buy the bicycle on credit. The salesman turned me over to his manager. The manager wanted to know how much I could pay down on the price of the bicycle. I said, *"Sir, I just came to live with my mother. I don't have any money. I desperately need this job, but they won't hire me unless I have a bicycle."* That kind manager let me ride that bike out of the store with no money down and a promise to pay him two dollars a week. I, also, picked up odd jobs here and there, such as, delivering circulars for Western Union and working part time for a small café. I gave most of my income to my mother.

One of our fellow paper route boys came in almost every morning to the station carrying a bag of oranges, apples or a bunch of bananas for everyone to enjoy. We thought he was very generous until we came upon him one morning and found out where he was getting them. There was a fresh air market that had a hole in their fence. He was reaching through that hole and helping himself to their fruit.

On this particular day he had just pulled a bag of oranges out and placed them in his bicycle basket, when we rode around the corner and met a policeman that we called Mr. Ed. This boy with the stolen oranges rode right by the officer and said, *"Good morning, Mr. Ed."* Mr. Ed said, *"Good morning, boys"* without even seeing the oranges.

On our paper routes, we were required to place all papers on porches or inside screen doors. One very cold morning at about five o'clock, I was riding my bicycle to where the papers were delivered for me to pick up. I would fold and pack them into my carrying bag for delivery. There was a heavy frost, and I was walking the pedals when my foot slipped off the pedal. I went over the handlebars with my gloves getting caught on the bars. My face was the first part of me to hit the ground. Fortunately, I didn't break my nose or knock any teeth out, but my face was very painful and full of black cinders. The frost had made my shoes slick, which had caused me to crash. I finished my route, but when I got home, I felt terrible. So, I missed that day of school. Not only was I hurt, but I was also embarrassed by this accident.

Youthful Capers

I was introduced to several of Roy's friends who became my friends, too. Where you saw one of us, the others were usually not far away. We were jokesters, but we never got into any serious trouble. There was a family that owned a community grocery store, which was next to the very large house where they lived. In their backyard was a huge pecan tree. We would sneak in their back yard and help ourselves to some of their pecans. They had a high fence that one of us would get across. Once across the fence, the next obstacle would be to climb up in the tree and shake the limbs that reached over the fence. The rest of us would pick up the pecans that were shaken down.

On school break one day, Roy was picking up pecans when one of the other boys threw a brick up in the tree to knock some of the pecans off the limbs. The brick hit another limb and bounced back down, striking Roy on the front part of his head. Everyone was frightened, because his head was bleeding badly. Not knowing what to do, he went on to school and told the nurse that he had been running and had fallen down, hitting his head on something hard. She cleaned up the wound and dressed it for him.

On a Halloween night, we would watch different houses until the lights would go out. Then, we would take a roll of scotch tape and several flexible sticks that we had cut, and sneak up to the doorbell to these houses. We would place one of the sticks over the doorbell, tape it down and then run off to watch. The lights would come back on, the front doors would open and the sticks would be yanked off the bell. Sometimes, the people would laugh and other times they would become very angry.

Around eleven o'clock on this Halloween night, we came to this particular house that had a rather tall pecan tree that was loaded with large pecans. Thinking everyone was in bed, a boy named Bill Huffman said, *"You guys watch, and I will climb up the tree and shake the pecans loose for you to pick up."* He shook that tree causing the nuts to fall down like rain, and we were picking them up by the handfuls.

Suddenly, a car whipped in the driveway, and the owner quickly jumped out of it. We all scattered except for Bill Huffman. However, just over the man's head, Bill had swung down off the limb and was holding on in midair by his hands. He held on to the branch as long as he could. Finally, he dropped just barely missing the owner, who was so startled that he just stood there for a few seconds. When Bill hit the ground, he hit it running, and that man soon lost sight of us all.

We lived on a busy street where many pedestrians constantly walked, because they did not own automobiles. As a prank, we would take two cans and put a hole in each one at the top. We, then, would put one can on each side of the sidewalk with a wire stretched from can to can. Filling these cans with water, we would hide and watch as the next person would come along and trip those cans causing the water to dump on their feet.

Mom put a curfew on us, which made us have to come inside early. However, many times we would go to our room, go out the window onto the roof and climb down a pear tree. We thought we were really cool. But, one night we started up to our room, and mom said, *"By the way, boys, I decided to switch bedrooms with you, so you go to the back bedroom."* We wondered if someone had tipped her off about us slipping out the window. We wanted to ask her why she switched bedrooms with us, but we did not dare.

Nearly Drowned—In a Fight & Then Friendship

One real warm day in late spring four of us boys went out to Lake Hickory, rented a boat, rowed out a good-ways and began diving off the boat. Suddenly, I don't know what happened, but it seemed impossible for me to move due to stomach cramps. I yelled, *"Help me, I'm drowning."* The others thought I was acting silly and just laughed until I started going down for the third time. One of the fellows said, *"He is drowning! Let's get him!"* They dived in, got me onto the boat and rowed fast to shore. All three of these guys were boy scouts. They laid me on the ground and pumped a lot of water out of me. Finally, I was able to sit up. Everything seemed to be all right except that I had a terrific headache.

Later, we went back to the river to a private place to go swimming. We stripped off to our birthday suit and were having a great time. Suddenly, we had company. Six black boys showed up to go swimming, also. They said, *"We will wait until you fellows leave."* We said, *"No! Strip down and come on in. There is plenty of room in this river."* They did, and we all had a great time. Back in those days, there was segregation, which was a curse to our nation. From my youth I always hated it, because I had many friends that were black.

The weather was beginning to become quite warm as we were getting close to the end of the school year. On this particular day after school, I was sitting on the ground leaning back against a tree. I was talking with several other students, when a friend by the name of Jim Sigmon rode up on his bicycle. Jim said, *"I'm going to run over your foot."* I said, *"Jim, I don't think that is a good idea, and I'm advising you not to try it."* He said, *"Yes, I am."* And he did.

I jumped up and we went at it, throwing punches at each other. We had been swapping blows for a while. All of a sudden, Jim reached down and picked up a large rock. He handed it to me and said, *"Go ahead, hit me with it—I dare you!"* I drew back, dropped the rock and hit him with full force right in his eye with my fist. Until the day a few years later when he became so despondent that he committed suicide, he would swear that I hit him with that rock.

I was really shocked when I received the news of his death and hated this very much. Jim and I were really long-time friends. In those days when we would get upset with one another, we would just fight it out. We just used our fists, and when the fight was over, we became friends again. In fact, we became greater friends after that fight and spent much time double dating and going many places together.

If I had hit him with that rock that day, he would have died sooner than he did. I don't know how long this fight would have gone on, but someone got word to my mother. She waded into the crowd that had gathered and said, *"Ralph, you come home now."* I respected mom and followed her home, but it took me quite a while to cool off.

Roy and I spent quite a bit of time at the Lenoir Rhyne College ball field playing ball. We were big fans of the Hickory Rebels, our local ball team, and this was their playing field. The night after Jim and I had fought that previous afternoon, Roy and I had attended a game and were on our way home when we met Jim. I figured the fight might be continued, but we passed each other with neither one of us speaking. When Jim got past me, he looked back and hollered, *"Hey Ralph! How are you?"* I said, *"I'm fine, Jim. How about yourself?"* He said, *"I'm okay except for this black eye."* He apologized for running over my foot, and I told him that I was sorry for giving him a black eye.

Wonderful Month on Another Farm

When I was fifteen years of age, I rode my bicycle to Maiden, North Carolina to visit my favorite aunt by the name of Victoria, my dad's sister. I stayed with her for a month and worked on her farm. It was truly an enjoyable time as I was treated royally. I did a lot of different kinds of work on her farm, but the most enjoyable was to plough with a blind mule. He was very obedient and depended on me for his eyes. My uncle Abe Ikerd informed me not to let the mule run into anything, because the mule would never trust me again.

It was very interesting to go with my uncle and aunt on Friday evenings to shop at a store where many farmers would gather. There were no strangers there, because everyone was known throughout this area. A family by the name of Sigmon owned a dairy farm that joined the farm of my uncle and aunt. I became good friends with a couple of their sons. Saturday nights would be our movie nights. My uncle would give me fifty cents, and I would go with these boys to the movies. Fifty cents paid my way into the movie and bought a box of popcorn.

There was enough money left over to buy a sandwich and a soft drink on our way home.

Narrow Escape Ends Tricks

Back in Hickory, we resorted to our mischievous tricks. One of these tricks almost got us in real trouble. Four of us were coming home from the movies when this wild idea came up in our thinking about throwing persimmons at passing automobiles. We knew where a certain yard was that had a persimmon tree with very ripe persimmons, so we headed in that direction.

We went inside an old garage to be hid from anyone seeing us. When a car would go by, we would toss the persimmons from the door. However, we all threw persimmons at this one car when, suddenly, it stopped and backed up. We ran to another shed and climbed up into the attic. The driver jumped out of his car and chased us. When he got to the shed, he said, *"Alright, I've got you fellows. Come on out."*

We had a chain hanging out a back window and were able to escape down the chain. But, it didn't take long until our chaser figured it all out. He ran back to his car and began to cruise around.

We had run over to another street that was out of the way to our homes. Then, we saw the lights of an automobile turn in our direction. Bill Huffman said, *"That's him, and I'm out of here!"* He jumped a yard fence and disappeared around the back of a house. My two other friends and I knew that we had been seen, so we just walked on. The car pulled up alongside us, and the driver got out.

To our astonishment, we realized that we had thrown ripe persimmons at the automobile of a deputy sheriff and his family. His teenage daughter was in the back seat wearing a very fancy white dress with the windows down, and those persimmons had made quite a mess on that pretty dress.

The deputy wanted to know where we had been. We told him that we were on our way home from the movies. He said, *"What have you got in those boxes?"* We said, *"Popcorn, sir."* He said, *"Let me see those boxes."* We obliged, and he looked into each box and saw that it was really popcorn. Then, we told him where we lived, and he said, *"This is out of your way home. What is your purpose for going this way?"* We informed him that a friend who was a musician lived this way, and we were going to his house to have him play his guitar while we sang. We knew the friend would back us up. Reluctantly, the deputy sheriff let us go, but we knew that he really did not believe us.

There was a small community grocery store next to my mother's house that had a bench out front. The three of us sat there wondering what had happened to Bill Huffman, who had jumped the fence and run.

After a while, we heard someone coming up the street. As the person got closer, we realized that it was Bill. With every step he took, there was a swooshing sound. We asked him what had happened, and he said, *"When I ran behind that house in the dark, I didn't see their fishpond, and I fell head-first into the thing."* We all doubled over in laughter. He said, *"You can laugh, but I may not be alive after tonight when my dad gets through with me. My mother bought me this suit and when I was leaving the house this evening, she cautioned me to be very careful with my new suit."*

We all sat down on the bench and began to discuss our foolish actions, which we had thought would be fun. Now, we all felt terrible about the mess we had made on the dress of the deputy sheriff's daughter. They had all been dressed very nice for some special occasion. We all agreed that it was time for us to grow up and stop our foolishness, which we did. We decided that we had better leave well enough alone and from that evening, there were no more pranks committed by us.

Warming Up

Bill Huffman bought a B-model Ford, and he and I would double date together. The car was very nice. It ran well, but we would get very cold, because there was no heater in it. I got the bright idea that if we had a small kerosene heater, it would take care of our problem. Bill readily agreed with me, so I proceeded to ask mom if we could borrow her small heater. Mom said, *"I don't think that is a very good idea. It could be dangerous."* I persuaded her that we would be very cautious, and she reluctantly consented.

That night I was in the back seat with my date. We had the heater sitting on the floorboard in the back, also. We all commented on how thankful we were for the heat we were enjoying from the heater, but no one noticed the brown spot forming in the car's headliner until it began to smoke. Thankfully, the car was a four-door model, and we all bailed out. I was able to grab the heater as I went out, while Bill beat out the fire in the liner. That put an end to our comforting warmth, but instead of Bill getting upset, he began to laugh and, then, we all started laughing.

My First Automobile Purchase

In the early part of 1941, I was working at different jobs trying to make some money, but I couldn't seem to find a good job. One day, there was a large ad in the local newspaper seeking to enroll students into an arc welding school. The ad emphasized that there was a grave shortage of welders. I talked my mother into going with me to talk to the people. After meeting with them, my mother agreed for me to borrow the money to enroll in this school, which was located in Charlotte, North Carolina. I boarded in a rooming house in Charlotte and graduated from the welding school. We were informed that the shipyard in Wilmington, North Carolina was hiring welders.

I went home and was able to purchase a 1936 Chevrolet automobile. My brother and I along with two of our friends took my new purchase out for a test drive. We were traveling along on a very dark stretch of road, when suddenly the headlights shorted out that left us in total darkness. Thankfully, I stopped when I did, because we were on the edge of a steep drop-off. We were able to repair the lights and continue to my mother's house. When we arrived at her house, I pulled in next to a large tree in our front yard. Roy said that if there had been another coat of paint on the car, the bark would have been stripped off the tree.

Roy Standing Against Tree I Barely Missed–Automobile on Right

My First Real Job

A couple of friends and I, who had all graduated from the welding school, drove to Wilmington, North Carolina. All three of us were hired on my eighteenth birthday by the Newport

News Shipbuilding Company. They required us to go through eight weeks of their welding school, also.

Replica Boarding House Located at 2nd and Nunn Street, Wilmington, North Carolina: My Home 1941 – 1942. Presently it is a "Bed and Breakfast House"

We boarded at a house in Wilmington that was located at 202 Nunn Street. It was a huge four-story house. We were blessed to find such a nice place to live where they served delicious meals. In later years, this house burned to the ground. Another interested party purchased the lot and rebuilt this house as a replica of the former house even furnishing it with old antiques to make it authentic to its original time. Today, it is a beautiful Bread and Breakfast house.

In May of 2018 my son, Terry, and I went on a father and son trip which included Wilmington, North Carolina. We parked on the street in front of this house, and we sat there a while admiring this beautiful home. I said to my son, *"Let's go up and ring the doorbell. Maybe, they will give us a tour."* The gentleman that answered the door was very kind. When I told him that I used to board there in 1941, he was thrilled and invited us to come in. He willingly gave us permission to tour all four levels. It brought back so many memories to me of the good times, wonderful fellowship and excellent meals.

I felt blessed to be in Wilmington and to have a good job there. Wilmington was and still is a beautiful city, but I thought I would freeze that winter sitting in one place welding on those ships with the wind blowing off that water.

Extra! Extra! Read All About It!

On Sunday, December 7th, 1941, several of us guys had attended a movie theater in Wilmington. When we came out of the theatre, there was a paper boy yelling, *"Extra! Extra!"* We bought a paper and the large headlines read, ***"Japan Attacks Pearl Harbor."*** We sat up late into the night listening to the news on the radio, because we all just knew that this would put the United States in war.

Extra! Extra! Read All About It! "Japan Attacks Pearl Harbor"

In the spring of 1942, another fellow by the name of Brown and I left Wilmington and drove to Savannah, Georgia. We went to the employment office of a shipbuilding company. We were hired by this company that was building mine sweepers for the Navy. Savannah is a very old, but beautiful city, too. I liked everything about this city, and the weather there was much milder than it was in Wilmington. The only thing that I had a problem getting used to in Savannah was the odor from the pulp mill.

After working several months at this shipyard welding galvanized steel to wrought-iron steel, I really enjoyed working there and enjoyed the men I worked with. In fact, I truly hated to leave this shipyard, because everyone was so very nice to me. However, the fumes from that galvanized steel kept making me sick. After giving a notice and working a final two weeks, I left there and went to work at another shipyard in Savannah named Southeastern Shipbuilding Company, which was building all black metal Victory Ships.

I felt very fortunate to be able to land these good jobs after coming through the Great Depression as a child. I remember the false hopes that were promoted and believed during the U.S. Presidential campaigning of President Herbert Hoover. His slogan promised "a chicken in every pot and a car in every garage." He served as the president from 1929 through 1932. Without personal fault of him, those four years were the toughest of the Great Depression. In the rural areas, those days were very primitive. The only paved roads were main U.S. highways and city streets. The country roads were plain old dirt in dry weather and plain old mud when the winter rains and snow fell.

Most everyone that were farmers owned wagons. Mules or horses were the main means of travel. During this time, some folks had a very small cart pulled by one horse. They were known as "Hoover carts." They received this name, because of the hard times under President Hoover. There were very few people that could afford automobiles, which were usually T-model or A-model Fords. They were about the only kind that could travel through the mud. In the wintertime, the ruts would become very deep. Today, antique car shows or a parade of restored automobiles always inspire tender memories of my dad's old stripped-down T-model Ford.

Hoover Cart

I had registered for the draft with the armed services and knew, without very much doubt, that I would be receiving my greetings from Uncle Sam. In October of 1942, I decided to quit my job at the shipyard in Savannah, Georgia and go to my mother's house in Hickory, North Carolina. There was a gasoline station a short distance from where my mother lived. The owner asked me to take it over and manage it for him. I agreed and started immediately. The station had a very good business.

One evening my mother went to a grocery store across the street from the gasoline station. On her way home, she stopped in at the station. There were several customers in the station at that time, when in walked a community neighbor who was always complaining. Most people tried to avoid him, because of his attitude. As he came into the station, he sniffed and said, *"What is that I smell?"* That struck me the wrong way, and I said, *"I don't know, but I didn't smell it until you came in."* Mother said, *"Son!"* The other people had a good laugh.

On another evening three of us fellows went to a ball game. On the way back home, we stopped at the station to get a soft drink. I had a deck of cards, and all three of us each took a card to see who would pay for the drinks. There came a knock at the station door. When I looked up, there were two police officers standing at the door. I opened the door and let them come into the station. They wanted to know if everything was all right, and we assured them that all was well. One officer said, *"We saw you fellows in here gambling."* I said, *"No sir! We each just drew a card to see who would pay for the drinks."* He said, *"That is gambling!"*

These officers loaded all three of us into their patrol car and took us to jail. At the jail, we came before Chief Sigmon. I knew the chief. He was the grandfather of my friend, Jim. When the officers explained our case, the chief looked at us and said, *"You boys go home and be careful."* I managed the station for about three months. Then, I left there in good standing and went to work at a box factory that built wooden boxes.

On Saturday nights it was customary for some of us to gather at Hill's Café in Hickory just for fellowship. Several of us were standing out front on the sidewalk when, suddenly, a police officer by the name of Willis came charging out the café door. He was chasing a fellow that was really moving on. Most people did not care too much for this officer, and one of our group said, *"Hey, Willis, what's your hurry?"* Willis said, *"That fellow said that at exactly one o'clock he wants me to kiss his backside!"* Another fellow said, *"What's your hurry, Willis? You still have ten more minutes."*

While we were all laughing, suddenly, that café door flew open again and out came my brother, Roy, with a large fellow right behind him. They ran down the street and turned into an alley behind a fresh air market. I said, *"We better check this out and see what is going on."*

We met Roy coming out of the alley. I said, *"Where is that guy that was chasing you?"* Roy said, *"I was no match against him, so I wrapped a banana stalk around his head."* I asked Roy what this was all about. He said, *"I was clowning around with his girlfriend, and she started paying more attention to me than him, which caused him to get upset."* We left there, then, thinking it was wise to make ourselves scarce.

Regardless of Leadership
There Will Be Good Times and Bad Times

In 1933, Franklin Delano Roosevelt became President of the United States of America. Life in general was still rough during this time with most people still struggling. Under this new leadership, different programs were instituted, which helped the situation little by little as it opened up the way for new jobs. In the late 1930's, many jobs begin to open up in defense plants, because it appeared that war would be unavoidable by the way things were already taking place against our allies in Europe.

Then, on December 7th, 1941, the Japanese Navy without warning made a heavy onslaught against the United States Navy in Pearl Harbor, Hawaii. The United States declared war against Japan. Young men immediately began to volunteer for the armed services while older men and women responded to a call for employment in defense plants. I, as previously stated earlier in the story, had been working in a shipyard as a welder on new ships that were being built.

After resigning from the job at the shipyard and moving back to Hickory, I had several other jobs, which included a welding job at the Piedmont Wagon Company. A friend of mine worked at this company and wanted to leave, but jobs were frozen at this time. This meant that you could not leave the job unless you found someone that would take your place. I told him that I would help him out, so I quit the box company and took his place welding for the wagon company.

Two months after I had begun working at the Piedmont Wagon Company, several of my friends received their greetings to report for military service. I checked with my draft board and asked them to clear the way for me to go in that draft, also, which was only a week away. They informed me that it was not possible, because it was too short of a notice. I said, *"You have a phone, and if you really want to, it can be done."*

I was confident that I would receive my letter, so I proceeded to inform the Piedmont Wagon Company on Friday, April 2nd, 1943 that I would not be back, because Uncle Sam needed me. I was resigning from my job in order to serve my country in the U.S. military.

The bosses at the company became very angry that I was leaving and let me know that when I returned home from the service, I could never work for them again. That certainly did not break my heart, because I had no intention of ever working for them again. The draft board would not promise to take me in the draft, but on Saturday after I quit my job on Friday, I received my greetings of *"I want you"* from Uncle Sam.

In front of Hotel Hickory, all of us that were being drafted into the military loaded up on a touring bus on a Monday morning bound for Spartanburg, South Carolina. After a number of tests, the physical being the last one, the examiner said to me, *"Army or Navy?"* I was surprised that I had a choice and said in exclamation, *"Navy?"* He hit my paper with a large stamp and directed me to the group that I was to join. I was sworn into the United States Navy on April 7th, 1943. After a couple of months of sea duty, I was thankful that I was inducted into the Navy. I liked serving aboard ship.

President Roosevelt was my Commander-in-Chief. It was a pleasure to serve under his leadership. He served in this capacity as President of the United States for twelve years until his death in April of 1945. The ship I served on, the USS Fleming DE 32, was at sea in the Pacific when we received this sad news of his death.

Immediately after President Roosevelt's death, Vice President Harry S. Truman became President of the United States of America. Today, President Donald J. Trump, our 45th and current president, is the sixteenth United States President that has served in the White House since I was born. So, over one third of the United States Presidents have served during my lifetime.

Delayed After Being Sworn into The Navy

After being sworn into the U.S. Navy, we were sent home for seven days. A group of us fellows went out on Saturday night to celebrate. On a Sunday morning, when I went into the kitchen, my mother started laughing. I said, *"Mother, what is so funny?"* She said, *"Son, go look in the mirror."* When I looked in that mirror, both of my jaws were sticking out like I had a golf ball in each cheek. I said, *"Mom, what is wrong with me?"* She said, *"Son, you have the mumps."* I said, *"Great!*

I am supposed to leave in the morning for the Navy." Those mumps got into my back and were very painful. A neighbor said, *"Ralph, you need to be seen by a doctor, and I know one that will come out and see you."* The doctor did come, and he put me to bed with my feet elevated and told me to stay there for a week. He informed me that this was very serious, and if care was not taken, it could ruin my life. The doctor, then, notified the Navy concerning my condition, and I received a letter from the Navy Department informing me that when all was clear, I should report in for duty.

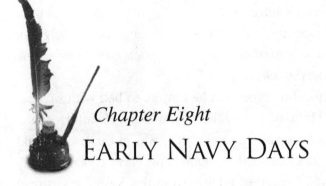

Chapter Eight
EARLY NAVY DAYS

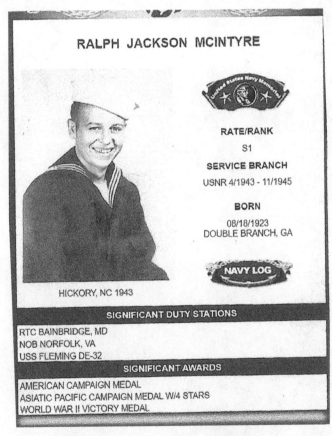

RALPH JACKSON MCINTYRE

RATE/RANK
S1

SERVICE BRANCH
USNR 4/1943 - 11/1945

BORN
08/18/1923
DOUBLE BRANCH, GA

NAVY LOG

HICKORY, NC 1943

SIGNIFICANT DUTY STATIONS

RTC BAINBRIDGE, MD
NOB NORFOLK, VA
USS FLEMING DE-32

SIGNIFICANT AWARDS

AMERICAN CAMPAIGN MEDAL
ASIATIC PACIFIC CAMPAIGN MEDAL W/4 STARS
WORLD WAR II VICTORY MEDAL

Ralph Jackson McIntyre In Uniform

A t the end of April in 1943 I was able to report to the Navy Department. There was a group of us loaded on a train and sent to Bainbridge, Maryland for boot camp training. When we arrived at camp around noontime, I was very hungry. We were marched to the chow hall. As we went through the line, we were served by other sailors. I like mustard greens and when they were placed on my plate, I requested another helping. The server looked at me as though he thought I was crazy, but honored my request. When we were seated at our table, my mouth was watering. I took a large bite of those greens, and I knew immediately that I was in trouble. There was a very large sign saying, *"Take all you want, but eat all you take."*

There was a very tough looking sailor standing by the area where the emptied trays were deposited. He was keeping a check on all of the trays. I did not like spinach, and I found out quickly that what I thought was mustard greens was spinach. With a plate full of spinach and not able to get rid of them, I went over to a condiment table to doctor those buggers up. It is amazing what vinegar and hot sauce can do. In fact, it was not bad at all. From that time on until this day, I truly enjoy spinach.

Leaving the mess hall, we were indoctrinated in the afternoon. We were given a lot of "can" and "cannot" instructions. Smoking was permitted only at certain times and places, taps (lights out) was 10:00 PM and reveille was 5:00 AM.

The next morning after breakfast we were all marched to the barber shop. When the barbers were finished with us, we left there looking like Geronimo had gotten a hold of us and scalped us—talk about skinheads, we were genuine skinheads. Some of the fellow's hair was full and wavy. I heard the barbers ask some of those guys, *"Do you want to keep your hair and sideburns?"* They answered, *"Yes!"* The barbers said, *"Hold out your hand."*

Our training was diversified—marching, running, drilling, double-timing, boxing, swimming, obstacle course, boat drills and hiking. When we boxed, we were paired with someone close to our size. Our chief said, *"I want you to box and not fake it."* My boxing partner said, *"If you won't hit me hard, neither will I hit you hard."* We were making a real good show until my partner cold-cocked me, which nullified our agreement. Our next round I waded into him with some hard punches, and he said, *"I thought we agreed to go easy on each other."* I said, *"That ended with the last round."*

Early every Saturday morning, we marched about a mile to the Susquehanna River for boat drills. Eight sailors were assigned to each rowboat (four on each side), and we would race each other down the river and back. We had to work harder on the return trip, because we were going against the current.

When we left the river, we were marched directly to the mess hall where it was almost impossible to eat, because of the heat. After lunch, we had to dress and be on the drill field at 1:00 PM for Regimental Parade where there was a lot of brass (officers) observing.

One Saturday it was so hot that there was an ambulance on each corner of the field, because now and then a sailor would pass out. Our chief looked around and saw that I was reeling back and forth. Before I went down, he ordered me to break rank and ordered another sailor to fall out and go with me back to the barracks.

Our swimming pool time was enjoyable most of the time. The pool was very long and at the deep end, there was a diving board forty feet plus above the water. We had to climb up to the board with full dress, including our helmet, and jump into the pool, because that was the height of World War Two aircraft carriers. Whether you could swim or not, you had to jump. They had a pole that they would reach out to the non-swimmers. We were taught many safety features in case we had to abandon ship. If you could not swim, you were given lessons instead of going to the obstacle course. Another sailor and I pretended that we could not swim, and we were enjoying escaping the obstacle course. Everything was going great until one particular day when we got caught. We thought our instructor was gone, and we were swimming around the pool and chasing each other when he reappeared. From that time on, it was the obstacle course for us. Along with these duties, we had rotating four–hour watches to stand.

Having completed "boot training" at the Naval Training Base in Bainbridge, Maryland, we were granted a seven-day leave. After boot camp, those seven days of leave granted to me were seemingly the fastest days of my life. When you are enjoying life, it appears as though time absolutely flies right on by.

After returning from leave, we were placed in the "Outgoing Unit" (OGU) for approximately two weeks. The chief for our company had us to fall in for muster. He was fully military, and we thought we were really going to have a hard time with him. He marched us along a trail into a deep part of the woods and called a halt. He said, *"Men, fall out and light up."* We sat around for a couple of hours while he told us interesting stories about the Navy. He looked at his watch and said, *"Men, it will be chow time when we march back, so fall in."* So, we went back to camp military style.

We left Bainbridge by train and ferry to the Naval Operating Base (NOB) in Norfolk, Virginia for assignment and further training. Our assignment was to serve aboard a recently launched ship at Mare Island, California. We traveled the southern route by train to California in time to participate in the commissioning of the "USS Fleming DE-32," a destroyer escort, on September 18th, 1943.

Our railroad cars that we traveled in were converted cattle cars. Bunks that we slept in were three high and they folded against the side for daytime travel. The weather was scorching hot, so we kept our windows open. However, this allowed black cinder dust to come in on us and truly change our appearance. When we arrived in Yuma, Arizona, the temperature was over 100 degrees. There were several blocks of ice on the train station platform, and the sailors bailed off the train and started chipping away at that ice. How refreshing!

In California, we sailors were warned by our Officers against going on liberty alone in the surrounding cities due to a group there called the Zoot-Suiters. I think another name fitting for them would be "Draft Dodgers." The suit they wore was called "Zoot-Suit." It was a man's suit of a former exaggerated style with high-waisted baggy trousers narrowing at the cuffs and a long draped black coat. Their custom also as part of their dress was a link chain down one side, which was a weapon they fought with. They were hideous in their appearance and ideology.

USS Fleming DE 32 Commissioning

These destroyer escort ships that we were assigned to were rather small. Their dimensions were 289 feet in length and 35 feet in width. They carried a crew of two hundred men. Both in the Atlantic and the Pacific, these little ships performed beyond everyone's expectations. They were referred to as *"Slim, but Deadly."*

Slim, but Deadly

"The largest number of warships ever built to a common design. America's bantam–sized destroyer escorts sank more enemy submarines than any other type of escort. Manned by more than 120,000 American and British sailors, the 563 destroyer escorts built gave allied navies a versatile, effective and deadly warship that served."

A person had to be twenty-one years of age to patronize the bars and night clubs. There was about a dozen of us that got the bright idea to alter our ID cards to show that we were of the proper legal age to be allowed to go to these places. They were done professionally, but for some reason it was discovered that one of the crew had the wrong date on his card. All ID cards were checked against everyone's records, and our secret was no longer a secret. We were all summoned to "Captain's Mass," which we all feared.

At this meeting the captain gave us a lecture that we did not forget, making us aware of how serious the charge was. He was lenient with the group by giving us extra duty with no liberty until all the duty was completed. He, then, stated that this would be placed in our records, but if we did not come back before him again, our records would be cleared in six months. I made sure that was the last time I appeared at a "Captain's Mass."

A laundry in Vallejo, California had granted three of us—Howard Lane, Ben Akridge and me—permission to spend time with them to learn the work in order that we might operate the laundry aboard ship. It was fun working in the laundry, because we were practically our own boss with no watches to stand. We could, also, make a few extra dollars by pressing dress uniforms when in port. When we left the United States, the officers sent down a number of nice white shirts to be laundered and pressed. After we had laundered the shirts, Ben said, *"We have to put some bluing in the water to make them white."* Howard and I didn't know anything about bluing. Ben said, *"I know how to do it, because I saw my mama do this many times."* Ben put the bluing in. When we went to take the shirts out of the washing machine, they were a sickly purple. We bleached those shirts until we got them white again, but there was a problem.

We had to be very careful folding them without them tearing. Ben said, *"Oh, don't worry! By the time they need these shirts again, they will think they have a bad case of dry-rot from the humidity."* We never heard any more about them.

Sailing to Join Combat Fleet

After completing our "shake-down" cruise to San Diego, California and back, an announcement over the PA system caused a surge of adventure in my heart. The announcer spoke these words, *"Now, set the special sea and anchor detail—all hands to quarters for leaving port."* We departed from Treasure Island, California and sailed under the Golden Gate Bridge on December 1st, 1943 with Pearl Harbor as our destination. We had an eager, but green, crew who had been waiting for the chance to get under way.

For those of us who served on destroyer escorts, it was hard to tell whether we were on a surface ship or a submarine when the seas were rough. I was seasick all the way to Pearl Harbor, because we were traveling through waves that were thirty to forty feet high. In fact, I slept top side in the spud locker, because every time I looked below deck and saw the bulkheads rolling, I became sick all over again.

The ship's cook said, *"Mac, you have got to eat something,"* and he gave me some crackers and cheese, which I was able to handle. It took me about thirty days to get my sea legs. I am thankful that I got used to the rolling and pitching, because sometimes we had very heavy seas. We had straps that fit across us in our bunks to keep us from being tossed from our bunks onto the deck.

USS Fleming DE 32 Screening for Enemy Submarines

After serving in the laundry room aboard the USS Fleming for seven months, I was assigned by personal request as "Jack-of-the-Dust." In this position, I had keys to the food storage. My responsibilities were to supply the cooks and bakers with supplies each day for cooking and baking. I held this position for two months before there was an opening for a baker's assistant.

The baker asked me, *"Would you like to learn baking?"* He said, *"Think it over and let me know."* After some thought, I decided that I would take the job; therefore, I moved into this position.

After approximately three months, the baker that trained me had to be taken out of the galley, because he had contracted a fungus on his hands that consisted of water blisters. From that point on, I was assigned a helper, and he and I did all the baking aboard the USS Fleming.

We had twelve black sailors that took care of serving the officers aboard the ship. One of these fellows from Kentucky by the name of Thompson was the officers' cook. He and I became good friends, and he was a very good cook. He always fixed excellent meals on Sundays. Since I had to do all of my baking at night due to the cooks having the galley in the day-time, I slept till around 2:00 PM. Then, I would go up to the galley on Sundays, and Thompson would say, *"Mac, I saved your meal."* He always put it in the warming closet, and it was always a tremendous meal.

These black sailors had their own sleeping quarters separate from the white sailors, but at battle stations we all had a job to fulfill. Our lives depended on each other. They were as loyal as anyone else, but at other times, sad to say, segregation was the order of the day. Thank God, that has changed! Today, they are recognized as equal human beings.

During my time as "Jack-of-the-Dust," a Navy buddy came to me with a request. He said, *"I need some grapefruit juice, sugar, yeast, raisins and several other ingredients."* I inquired as to why he needed all these supplies. He said, *"It is best that you do not know."* I filled his request and found out later that these ingredients were used to make a keg of "Raisin Jack," an alcoholic beverage. I found this out after he handed me a cup of the brew. While fermenting, it gave off quite an odor, but they had it in the storage area in the bow of the ship where no one ever checked.

One sailor by the name of Corky, who was part American Indian and rather small in stature, slipped down to that locker one evening while a movie was being shown on the fantail (aft) of the ship, and he got highly intoxicated on that "Raisin Jack." Then, he came up on the quarter deck and pulled out his sheath knife. He threw it past the Officer of the Day, and it stuck in the top of the desk. Corky said, *"Who wants to fight?"* They had to put him in the lockup. Then, the officers were trying to figure out how Corky had gotten an alcoholic beverage in the middle of the Pacific Ocean.

I was called to the quarter deck, because I had the keys to all areas including the beer locker. I was asked if I had given any beer to anyone, and my reply was, *"No, sir!"* An officer accompanied me to the storage area and took inventory of our stock. He found that the beverage was all accounted for. That episode remained a mystery, because everyone remained mum.

After training in the Hawaiian Islands, the USS Fleming sailed for Tarawa, Gilbert Islands (now known as Kiribati Islands) on January 15th, 1944, where she did local patrol and escort duty. There were seventy-five marines still in Tarawa from the invasion, and they were needed for the invasion of Kwajalien, Marshall Islands. Therefore, our ship was designated to transport them.

They were crowded into close quarters and we were traveling through rough waters. Most of the marines became seasick. One of the marines said, *"I don't know how you fellas can stand to ride this ship. I would much rather be on land and facing the enemy."* We continued escort missions in the South Pacific from Funfuti, Tuvalu Islands – Kwajalien and Majuro, Marshall Islands – and Makin, Gilbert Islands (Kiribati) through April.

Return to Pearl Harbor

We only made a couple of return trips to Pearl Harbor, but we were always thrilled when over the PA system they announced that we would be making port in that harbor again. The USS Fleming returned to Pearl Harbor on May 19th, 1944 for a brief overhaul. The Royal Hawaiian Hotel was leased to the Navy department. Those with submarine duty had priority to receive a few days there for R & R (rest and relaxation).

When we arrived at Pearl Harbor, there were no submarines in port, so our ship was granted a three-day stay there. It had the right name, because we were treated "Royal." The food was superb, and it was great to just get into the bathtub and soak for a while. That was the first time I ever saw a bathtub sunk so deep that the top of the tub was even with the floor. In those days, Hawaii was much different from what it is today.

Hawaii was not a state during World War Two. It had its own government and governor or king. Young women were solicited in the states to go to Hawaii and serve as prostitutes for the military. There was a number of brothels throughout Honolulu, and although they displayed no signs, a person could tell where they were by the lines of mostly Navy personnel waiting their turn.

The ruler of the Islands decided that this was degrading to the Hawaiian Islands, so he gave notice that on a certain date he was driving all of the girls out of town and shutting all brothels down. Our ship was in port when this took place, and the reporters wrote it up big time. They placed a picture in the paper of young girls running down the street robed in just a towel with police officers chasing them with "Billy" clubs.

Leaving Pearl Harbor on June 7th, 1944, The USS Fleming sailed for Eniwetok, Marshall Islands, where she joined a convoy bound for newly assaulted Guam. The USS Fleming patrolled off Orote, Guam and escorted merchantmen from Guam to Tinian, Northern Mariana Islands and Eniwetok, Marshall Islands.

On August 20th, 1944, she escorted an attack transport to Saipan and, then, proceeded on to Pearl Harbor to be put in dry dock. The USS Fleming was in dry dock for sand blasting and painting the bottom of the ship. During this time, our crew was given a retreat at a place called Camp Andrews, which was enjoyed by all. The USS Fleming acted as a target for submarine training in Hawaiian waters until October 17th, 1944. She left port and arrived at Eniwetok, Marshall Islands to begin four months of uninterrupted convoy escort duty between Eniwetok and Ulithi, Falatop Island in Micronesia. This Island was the great base where buildup was essential to the forthcoming Iwo Jima and Okinawa operations.

Ralph (On Right)
Strolling Down Waikiki Beach
With Two Shipmates

**The Fleming Sank Japanese Submarine and
Splashed (shot down) Two Enemy Planes.
Japanese Flags Displayed on Ship's Smokestack.**

Contact with Japanese Submarine

On the night of January 13th, 1945, guarding two tankers
in route from Ulithi to Eniwetok, the USS Fleming made
radar contact with an unidentified surface craft at a distance
of approximately seven miles. The USS Fleming moved to the
area at full speed to investigate. At a distance of three miles
we challenged the craft with a signal light, but got no response.
The radar screen went blank. This was evidence that it was a
submarine, and it had crash-dived. The USS Fleming raced to
the spot and began her five hedgehog and depth charge attacks,
which sank the Japanese submarine I-362. The blast shook the

USS Fleming and damaged her sound gear. We rejoiced that we had been able to get them before they got us.

By daybreak, an oil slick fifteen miles in length and half a mile wide had developed. The oil was still bubbling to the surface in water that was more than three miles deep. After numerous attempts to obtain samples of oil for tests in naval laboratories, a boat was put over the side to collect as much of the coagulated oil as possible. A Navy pilot flew his plane low over the area and verified the large area of oil.

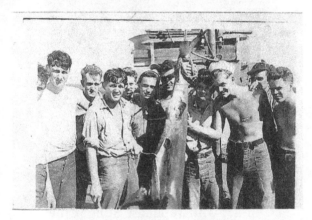

Shark Butcher Shop....... DE–32 Fantail

At first, schools of sharks were ignored until one of the more abstract minds thought there might be evidence in the sleek, gray bellies of the man eaters. Grappling hooks and bait were broken out, and in less than two hours six sharks had been pulled aboard. None of these sharks were less than five feet in length. Their stomachs were removed, and upon examination, they were found to contain partially digested flesh with some small pieces of metal. These specimens were returned to the United States for analysis. In the official records, the USS Fleming was listed as having severely damaged and sunk the Japanese submarine.

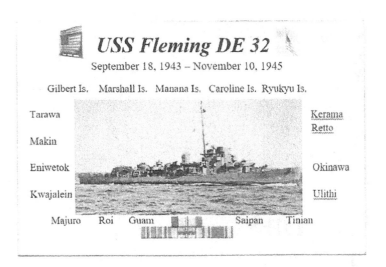

USS Fleming DE 32
September 18, 1943 – November 10, 1945

Gilbert Is.   Marshall Is.   Manana Is.   Caroline Is.   Ryukyu Is.

Tarawa	Kerama Retto
Makin	
Eniwetok	Okinawa
Kwajalein	Ulithi

Majuro   Roi   Guam   Saipan   Tinian

**Ralph Jackson McIntyre Served Aboard the USS Fleming DE 32
During Her Tenure of Twenty Months in the Pacific.
We Took Active Part in the Islands Listed Above**

Chapter Nine
WORLD WAR TWO'S LAST, BUT BLOODIEST BATTLE

I n late February and early March of 1945, the USS Fleming made escort voyages in the Pacific from Eniwetok to Saipan and Guam. The following dates are in 1945 unless specifically stated.

On March 13th, we arrived at Ulithi to prepare for the Okinawa assault. On March 21st, the USS Fleming was under way as part of a Task Unit of fifteen ships including five aircraft carriers (CVEs). The Task Unit was in route from Ulithi to Ryukyus Islands to participate in Operation Iceberg, which was the invasion of Okinawa. This was the last great battle for destroyer escorts in WWII. During the afternoon of March 25th, three mines were sighted and destroyed. One mine was destroyed by the USS Fleming and two mines were destroyed by two other units in the screen.

On March 26th, the USS Fleming was assigned to another Task Unit of twenty ships including eight carriers. On March 31st, a plane from Petrof Bay (CVE-80) crashed on takeoff. The USS Fleming rescued Ensign Robert H. Allison, USNR pilot, who was in good shape except for a large knot on his head where he hit the panel. Petrof Bay had loosed a life raft, which Ensign Allison had reached. When we arrived, he was sitting on the raft looking down at sharks swimming around him. We transferred him and the raft back to his mother ship. On April 1st, which was both Easter Sunday and April Fool's Day, was the date chosen to attack the beachhead. Our ships bombarded the island very strongly with their large guns, and our Navy flyers made heavy bombing raid after raid on these islands for two weeks.

At times our ship was ordered closer to the shore at night to fire star shells that lit up the area. This was to assist the cruisers and battle ships in hitting their target. They had the eight, fourteen and sixteen-inch shells that they fired across our ship to hit the island. Our ears were affected by the noise from these big guns.

Kamikaze (suicide plane) attacks of April 1st and 2nd scored hits on fifteen (15) of our ships. On April 5th, the USS Fleming sighted a four-horned type mine close to the port. We exploded the mine with .30 caliber rifle fire. From April 3rd through April 13th, an additional forty-one of our ships were damaged or sunk by the Kamikaze onslaught. We had a very busy afternoon on April 6, 1945 with 900 Japanese planes of which one third were kamikaze planes.

At 18:37 on April 13th, the USS St. Louis (CL-49) splashed a Val (Japanese suicide plane) which was approaching on the USS Fleming's starboard beam. It was estimated to have hit the water several hundred yards away after approaching out of the sun. The USS St. Louis saved the USS Fleming that day. Our radar had shut down; therefore, we were not aware that enemy planes were in the area. I came up from below deck in time to see the plane coming down in a ball of fire. Then, over the PA system, came the orders for everyone to man their battle stations. From that moment on, we had a very busy evening.

On May 17th, there were several "Air Flash Reds" or battle stations during the night. At 23:01, a bogie (enemy aircraft) was heard close by without warning. It passed down the starboard side under heavy fire from our starboard machine guns. Then, it passed over the fantail and disappeared. It was identified as a Val. My gun was a twenty- millimeter gun located next to the smoke stack on the starboard side of the ship.

On May 18th, we were granted permission to proceed to Kerama-Retto to pick up much needed supplies and to get a night's rest. This was an island of the Ryukyus group that was protected by smoke screens. When in port, guards with machine guns were stationed on the bow and stern, because sometimes hungry Japanese would swim out to our ships and search through the garbage for food.

On May 19th at 2:00 AM, my assistant and I were in the galley baking bread and pastries, when suddenly there was a loud noise accompanied by our ship being shook very hard. We thought that we had been hit by a kamikaze plane that had gotten through the smoke screen. We left the galley and went out on deck only to come face to face with another ship whose anchor had failed to hold. This ship had swung around and slammed into our ship. What a relief! And, there was no damage to either ship.

On May 20th at 18:33, we went to General Quarters (battle stations) for the first of the evening "Air Flash Reds." Ensign James T. Krause, Assistant Gunnery Officer, was next to our gun on a raised platform. He controlled the gun fire in our area aboard ship. I saw a plane coming straight toward our ship. I had the phone for our gun, and I said to the Gunnery Officer, *"Sir, that plane is heading straight for our ship."* The Officer replied, *"That's alright. It's a friendly plane."* I said again,

"Sir, that is an enemy plane, and he is still heading straight for our ship." He emphatically said again, *"It is a friendly plane!"* I told our gunner to be ready to fire at any moment, because that was definitely an enemy plane. Come to find out, it was a Kamikaze suicide plane headed straight for the USS Fleming, but, suddenly, veered away and headed for the USS Thatcher (DD-514) in the station next to our screening station. He dived into her just next to the bridge structure. I said to the Gunnery Officer, *"Sir, that friendly plane just dived into the USS Thatcher."* He did not appreciate that, but he deserved a more severe reprimand, because his lack of diligence could have cost many lives.

The USS Fleming proceeded toward her to offer our assistance until forced to maneuver away for her own protection from nearby bogies. At 20:20, an estimated three enemy planes made apparent suicide or bombing runs on our ship. Our guns were firing away when second loader, Riley Hodge, yelled at first loader, Hap Holladay, *"Hap, he's going to get us!"* Hap replied, *"Keep firing until he does."* Hap's gunner hit the plane, and it veered across the bow and down the starboard side. Our gunner began firing, and the enemy plane hit the water about a thousand feet from our ship. The USS Fleming gun crews splashed (shot down) two planes and one turned away. They were identified as "Zekes."

On May 23rd a patrolling screening station was assigned to the USS Fleming, and continuous raids came from the north through midnight with numerous enemy planes being destroyed. On May 25th at 02:47, we were completely straddled for several minutes by five-inch gun fire. Shrapnel and spray landed aboard the Fleming with some of it hitting the smoke–stack next to our gun, but fortunately there were no casualties. On

May 27ᵗʰ, there were two "Flash Reds," which brought heavy enemy air raids throughout the night.

Kamikaze Planes Kept Our Guns Busy

4 Barrel 1.1 gun

At 08:12, we received orders to proceed to another station to offer our assistance to ships damaged in that area. At 09:20, we arrived at the scene and found LSM-135 burning, settling and abandoned. At 09:58, we took aboard eleven survivors including the Executive Officer. Three of the survivors were stretcher cases. We, then, proceeded toward Le Shima to transfer survivors.

At 11:08, the USS Bates (APD-47) was hit westward of Le Shima by two suicide planes. The USS Bates was now burning fore and aft with the fires spreading rapidly. We were able to get alongside the USS Bates and take on twenty survivors with several being wounded. Several of the USS Fleming crew jumped overboard and rescued some of the USS Bates crew that were in the water. Our crew had to be careful where they touched these men, because they had been burned very badly.

Iva Toguri D'Aquino, known as Tokyo Rose, was born in Los Angles, California in 1916. Her father was Canadian and her mother was Japanese. After graduating from the University of California in Los Angles with a degree in Zoology, she was sent to Japan in July of 1941 to care for her mother's dying sister. Her mother, who was too ill to travel, died the following year on her way to a Japanese–American internment camp. Iva tried to return to the United States on December 2nd, 1941, but was refused entry into the country by American authorities.

Iva Toguri "Tokyo Rose," The "Siren of the Pacific"

Trapped while visiting Japan at the start of World War Two, U.S. citizen Iva Toguri became known to millions by a radio handle she never used: "Tokyo Rose, The Siren of the Pacific." Her radio broadcasts were meant to demoralize American servicemen fighting in the Pacific theater. But, the fact was widely known that she was not the only "Tokyo Rose" in existence. U.S. servicemen branded any English-speaking female radio broadcaster of Japanese propaganda with that name, and there were at least a dozen different broadcasters called "Tokyo Rose." Stranded and classified as an enemy alien, Ms. Toguri was constantly harassed by the Japanese government. Taunted by neighbors for harboring an enemy, her relatives asked her to leave. She asked Japanese authorities to imprison her with other American nationals, but she was eventually forced to work on the English-language Zero Hour, a Radio Tokyo show manned by allied prisoners that aired from 1943 to 1945.

The Japanese developed a way to demoralize the American forces. Psychological warfare experts developed a message they felt would work. They gave the script to their famous broadcaster, Iva Toguri, and every day she would broadcast the same message packaged in different ways, hoping it would have a negative impact on the morale of American GIs. This message had three main points: (1) Your President is lying to you, (2) This war is illegal and (3) You cannot win this war. She always included in her broadcast that she was on our side, too.

On board the USS Fleming, most of the sailors looked forward to her program. She would play western music and make remarks such as, *"Sailors, you are risking your lives, and some of you are dying while your wife or girlfriend back home is sitting under the apple tree with some other guy."* She, then, would announce the many ships that the Japanese Navy had sunk.

One day while we were on patrol duty, she announced that our ship, the USS Fleming DE 32, had been sunk. We got a charge out of that. After the war, she became the seventh woman in the USA to be tried and convicted for treason in 1949. She served six years in prison. Two decades after her conviction, journalists revisited her story and helped clear her name as a victim of racism and wartime hysteria. She refused to denounce her USA citizenship, although the Japanese tried to force her to do that. Ms. Toguri received a presidential pardon in 1977. She died September 26th, 2006 at age 90.

On May 27th, 1945 we were illuminated by flares dropped from a high altitude on parachutes. Fourteen separate flares were counted. The captain reduced speed by two-thirds. When activated and dropped from a plane, it is true that USA Mark-24 Model 3 parachute flares can provide up to two million candle-power of light for three minutes.

This tremendous light is created through a combination of magnesium and sodium nitrate, chemicals that were kept separate in the flare until a sharp pull on its lanyard mixed them. When ignited, the chemicals combined and burned furiously at a temperature of 4500 degrees. Furthermore, the chemical composition of the flare resisted all firefighting efforts once they were ignited. I don't know what chemicals were used in these Japanese flares, but they lit up the area like day for about five minutes, which made it too bright for comfort. As the last flare extinguished, the captain ordered full speed and a rudder change of course.

At 22:44, an unidentified enemy plane made a low approach on port bow. Our guns opened fire as they crossed the bow, causing them to turn away. Then, we heard two heavy explosions close enough to shake our ship, which we assumed to be bombs or torpedoes exploding. When the captain had ordered the engine speed cut by two-thirds, many of the sailors including me thought the "Old Man" (captain) had gone crazy. We felt like he was causing us to be sitting ducks for the enemy to pick us off. However, when the last flare went out and the captain ordered full speed with a rudder change of direction, we sailors realized that he knew what he was doing. The enemy was trying to chart our speed and direction to bomb us, but the change of speed and direction caused the explosives to miss us and hit near enough for us to feel the shaking of our ship. The captain's decision had, perhaps, saved our lives that night.

All these situations certainly played havoc with a fellow's nerves. I've seen real macho men on their knees calling on God. The majority of the sailors aboard ship smoked rather excessively at these times, although smoking was not permitted during General Quarters. Outside the Continental United States, we could purchase cigarettes at five cents a pack, and there was no warning concerning the health factor. We got paid every two weeks, and I would go to the ship's store to buy two cartons (20 packs) of Camel cigarettes for one dollar.

Okinawa's Deadly Campaign

From May 28th until July 5th, 1945, the USS Fleming patrolled radar picket duty at various stations around Okinawa, Le Shima and Kerama Retto, which were all in the Ryukyu Islands that were south of the four big islands of Japan. The Battle of Okinawa was the largest amphibious assault during the Pacific campaign of World War II. From the beginning, this battle was shaping up to be a very bloody campaign. It was the largest air–land–sea battle in history that actually lasted from April through June of 1945. World History documented this to be the worst air, land and sea battle in history.

After the capture of Iwo Jima in March of 1945, General Douglas MacArthur, Supreme Commander of the Southwest Pacific Area, turned his attentions to the island of Okinawa.

Lying just 563km (350 miles) from the Japanese mainland, it offered excellent harbor, airfield and troop-staging facilities. It was a perfect base from which to launch a major assault on Japan. Consequently, it was well-defended with 120,000 troops under General Mitsuru Ushijima who later took his own life. The Japanese also committed some 10,000 aircraft to defend this island.

The United States Navy assembled an unprecedented armada in April of 1945 with 1,300 ships lying in wait off the coast of Okinawa. In fact, the effort in the spring offensive of 1945 was far greater than the previous spring offensive in Europe.

During the Normandy invasion, the allies had employed 150,000 troops, 284 landing ships and 570,000 tons of supplies, all of which required a very short supply line. However, maintaining this supply line on Okinawa, in Japan's backyard, seemed like an incomprehensible feat. The landing force was under the leadership of Lieutenant-General Simon Buckner. But, just prior to June 21st, this great leader was killed from an exploded shell.

In the invasion of Okinawa, there were 183,000 troops, 327 landing ships and 750,000 tons of supplies. However, by the time the battle finished, more than 300,000 soldiers were involved in the fighting. This made it comparable to the Normandy landing in mainland Europe in June of 1944. The Okinawa landing, which was on Easter Sunday, April 1st, 1945, would be referred to as "L Day" or "Love Day." Of course, it was also April Fool's Day. The landing encountered virtually no opposition.

On the first day, 60,000 troops were put ashore at Hagushi. The following day the Americans captured two airfields.

However, when the soldiers reached Shuri, they came under heavy fire and suffered heavy casualties.

We were informed that the civilians of Okinawa were told that in order to be a U.S. Marine, the marines had to kill their own mother. Many of the Japanese military killed their families while others committed suicide, because they feared what they would face if captured by the Americans. Also, the Japanese soldiers turned their guns on many of the civilians.

Naval casualties in the Okinawa fighting were higher than any other Pacific campaign. U.S. Navy deaths were at 4,907, exceeding the number of U.S. Navy wounded of 4,824. There were 38 U.S. ships that were sunk, 368 ships that were damaged and a loss of 763 U.S. aircraft. There were 50 USS Destroyer Escorts that served on the Okinawa radar picket line. Out of these 50 vessels, there were 22 that were either damaged or destroyed by Kamikaze attacks. A total of 30 Japanese submarines were destroyed. The USS Fleming was one of the fortunate ships that avoided being hit.

One time during this campaign our food supplies were running low and weevils got into our flour. When we opened a bag, those little insects filled the galley. I reported this to our division officer and asked what we should do, although we thought he would say to throw it overboard. After checking with our doctor, the officer came back and said for us to go ahead, use the flour and bake the bread, because there was nothing in the weevils that would hurt anyone. There was no way to get those weevils out of the flour. After baking and slicing the bread, there those weevils were. It was comical to watch our shipmates try to pick out all the weevils. Finally, they just spread grape jelly on their bread and forgot about the weevils.

A message was sent out from a ship that had received orders to set sail for another destination, stating that they had several dressed Australian goats for anyone that could use the extra meat. Our disbursement officer sent a message to them that he would be more than happy to accept their offer. At the time, in my position, I had keys for all food and beverage storage. I despised goat meat, because of the way the cooks prepared it. I just could not force myself to eat it. The officer instructed me to place the goat meat in the cooler. Knowing he had misspoken and really meant for me to put the meat into the freezer, I was delighted to store it in the cooler. In a few days the fish had themselves a feast—it all spoiled and we had to throw it overboard.

The island of Okinawa was secured on June 21st, 1945. Okinawa was a battle of battles that never received the proper recognition it deserved. This was a disservice to those that participated, those who were disabled and especially to all those that paid the supreme sacrifice. I should know, because our ship was there through it all. I have copied the following history from documented history of Okinawa:

Ironically, because Okinawa was the final battle of the Second World War, the war's end obscured the battle's accomplishments. In 1945, Journalist Sid Moody of the Associated Press summarized it best when he stated, *"Before Hiroshima, there was Okinawa. Because of Okinawa, in considerable part, there was Hiroshima. Okinawa lost its place in history, in part, because of Hiroshima."*

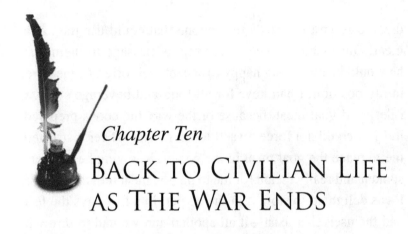

Chapter Ten

BACK TO CIVILIAN LIFE AS THE WAR ENDS

Homeward Bound

Then, on July 5th, 1945, the USS Fleming received orders to set sail for Pearl Harbor. From there, we were to proceed on to the states to undergo an overhaul and refitting to be part of the Task Unit that would participate in the planned invasion of Tokyo. At 14:30 on July 26th, 1945, we passed from international to inland waters. At 15:31, the USS Fleming moored portside to berth 5, pier 2, Astoria Harbor, in Astoria, Oregon. At 16:00 all hands commenced unloading ammunition.

Then, at 02:39 on July 27th, 1945, a river pilot came aboard, and we were underway traveling up the Columbia River. At 09:16, we moored starboard side to pier B, Municipal Terminal #1, Portland, Oregon. By this stage, the USS Fleming had served in the Pacific for twenty (20) consecutive months. Upon arrival in Portland, we received a 30-day leave, and I traveled by train to my mother's house in Hickory, North Carolina.

Tragedy Strikes the USS Indianapolis

While home on leave at the end of July of 1945, we received the news that the USS Cruiser Indianapolis, (the ship that transported the atomic bomb to the island of Tinian), was ordered to proceed to Leyte, Philippine Islands. Captain Butler McVay III requested escorts, but he was told that there were none, and he would have to proceed without them. Therefore, obeying orders, he got underway without any escorts.

On July 30th, 1945, a captain of a Japanese submarine spotted the Indianapolis and torpedoed this ship. She was sunk and took many brave sailors down with her. Those who survived the fiery sinking—some injured and many without life jackets—struggled to stay afloat as they waited to be rescued. But, the United States Navy did not even know they were missing.

It was the worst disaster in U.S. Naval history, and the Navy did not want to answer the most obvious question: *How could the United States Navy have failed to notice that the ship was missing for five days before being accidently discovered by a pilot on patrol duty?* Of the 1,197 crew members aboard the Indianapolis when she sailed for Leyte, only 317 survived. A large number of these men lost their lives by sharks.

The Navy needed a scapegoat, so they disgraced Captain Charles Butler McVay III by court-martialing him. Their excuse was to blame him for stopping the weaving of the ship, which he had ordered, because of the heavy dense fog. He thought it would be safer under the circumstances to do this. After the Navy charged him with the blame, Captain McVay III later committed suicide.

Several years passed when a young man by the name of Hunter Scott became very interested in this story and began his search for justice for the USS Indianapolis and Captain McVay

III. His work paid off with the final results ending in the exoneration of Captain McVay III. Many of the escort sailors had a very strong feeling of how different things would have possibly been if the USS Fleming or some other escort ships had been traveling with the USS Cruiser Indianapolis.

Atomic Bombs Dropped

In the latter part of July, Naval pilots began flying over the city of Hiroshima, Japan and dropping flyers of warning to the people that a disastrous bomb was going to be dropped on that city. But, they were ignored. On August 6th, 1945, the atomic bomb was dropped on Hiroshima; however, this did not bring the Japanese to the table of surrender. The flyers were also dropped on the city of Nagasaki. Likewise, these people paid no attention to the warning. On August 9th, 1945, the second bomb was dropped on Nagasaki.

There was a weighty feeling of sorrow and regret for all the civilians that were killed and the many that were severely injured, but that is the peril of war. These atomic bombs were what got Japan's attention causing them to come to the table of surrender. If the Japanese would have held out on surrender, and there had been an invasion of mainland Japan, the United States of America along with others would have lost thousands more of men than what they did.

At 18:00 (6:00 PM) on Tuesday, August 14th, 1945, President Harry Truman announced that Japan had accepted terms of defeat, thus beginning the process of bringing World War II to a close. The war was over. We that had survived this war felt very fortunate that we had lived through this most difficult time.

The United States Government awarded the USS Fleming DE 32, a Destroyer Escort, four (4) bronze battle stars for

World War II service. It is a shame that our present generation, as a whole, knows so little of what price the former generations have paid in order for them to have their present liberty.

USN Admiral Chester W. Nimitz Signs the Instrument of Surrender of Japan as United States Representative on Board the USS Missouri

Military Family

Shortly after I left home for the Navy, my brother joined the Army and served in Europe under General Patton. My brother was wounded in the Battle of the Bulge, which probably saved his life, because most of his company was killed. My sister, Lorene, joined the Waves (Navy) and served in Washington, D. C. during World War Two.

When I left home in July of 1943 after the expiration of my leave, I was away until July of 1945 when our ship returned to the States. From the time I left for the Navy, I did not see my brother for three years. When we met, it was a grand reunion.

Lorene served honorably in our nation's Capital as a secretary. We were a patriotic family and loved America very much. We count it a privilege to have honorably served our country.

Ralph – Lorene – Roy:
Military Service WWII

America Celebrates the End of World War Two

After President Truman made his announcement stating that the war was over, I was sitting in an automobile in front of a Navy buddy's house. The name of this buddy was Lewis Correll. Lewis came to the door with a big grin and a thumbs-up gesture. I think I probably had both hands raised. Sirens started screaming, factory whistles began sounding off, church bells could be heard ringing and car horns began blowing. An announcement came over the radio that factories and businesses were closing for the evening. People began congregating on the town square of Hickory, North Carolina.

After he finished dressing, Lewis came outside. We decided to go uptown to join the crowd. Once there, we parked our car and walked along with the great number of people that had already assembled. Two young ladies caught our eye, and we agreed together to go over and work our charm on them. Making our way through the mass of people, we finally got to where they were. I felt there was something special about this meeting, so we were very cautious in our approach. These girls were very skeptical of two sailors, but after we had talked for a while, they both consented to walk with us around the block along with the crowd. After spending about two hours with them, they agreed to let us drive them home.

When Ralph and Frances First Met

My Life Would Change

Frances Bonnie Houston, the lady that I was with, worked on the second shift and agreed to see me again on Saturday. At this meeting, we had a very enjoyable time. Then, a couple of weeks later her younger sister arrived to spend the weekend.

She was introduced to Lewis, and they hit it off from the beginning. We had two weeks of real enjoyment together.

Due to the war, gasoline and many other things were rationed, which means you had to have stamps in order to make a purchase. We could not go far on the small amount of gasoline stamps awarded to us; however, Lewis had a farmer friend with extra stamps, and I had a friend that ran a service (gasoline) station who had extra stamps, so we were well equipped to travel to see these girls.

When our leave time ended, Lewis and I both had to head back to Portland, Oregon, which we did reluctantly. Although I had never felt as comfortable about any girl as I did this one, no thought ever crossed my mind that she would change my life for good by becoming my wife. We wrote to each other often over the next three months.

Sailors Frolic

Back in Portland, Oregon, we were rather busy during the day, because our ship had been ordered to be decommissioned. In the evening, we usually had liberty unless we had to stand watch. Everybody in Portland was very nice and friendly to us.

We started going out to night clubs and bars more and more until we were drinking excessively. One night I was out with two shipmates when one of them by the name of Charlie McCarthy over indulged and became intoxicated. Another shipmate, James Norton, and I had him by each arm and were taking him back to the barracks we had moved into. As we were passing in front of a theatre, Charlie suddenly leaned back and stuck both feet through the theatre plate glass window. A police cruiser stopped, and two policemen bailed out and took hold of Charlie. Charlie started to fight with them, and one policeman started to draw his pistol. I said, *"Charlie, that officer will shoot you."* The officer said, *"You got that right."* In moments, a paddy wagon pulled to the curb, and all three of us were transported to jail.

When the paddy wagon arrived at the station, I asked the policeman where I could find a rest room. He said, *"It is downstairs."* Downstairs I went with the officer right behind me. When we came back upstairs, there was a Navy SP (Ship's Police) who was well over six feet tall standing with my shipmates. Charlie had a real bruiser on his left cheek, and the SP instructed me to get on the elevator with them. We were taken to the third floor and placed in a cell, which was our home for the night. I asked what had happened to Charlie's face. James said, *"He tried to take on the SP.... end of story."*

The next morning we were brought before the judge. He pointed his finger at James Norton and me saying, *"I have dropped charges against these two sailors. They are free to go."* When Charlie was brought in, the judge reprimanded him and fined him fifty dollars to repair the theatre window. This happened the day after payday, so my shipmate and I went back to the barracks and asked the crew to contribute until we had collected the fine. We, then, took it to the court, and Charlie was released. We were a little embarrassed when the newspaper came out, and we read, *"Sailors Frolic"* with an account of what had happened including the listing of our names.

On another occasion, several of us sailors wound up into a ruckus with another group of sailors from another ship. After things settled down, and we were leaving the establishment, one of the sailors thought we were stalking him, which was not true. When we drew quite close to him, suddenly, he whirled around and we were looking down the barrel of a Navy forty-five automatic pistol. He said, *"If you think I won't shoot, just one of you take one step and you will see."*

We were all shocked. I don't think I could have moved if I had wanted to. Finally, we persuaded him that we just happened to be going the same direction he was, and we were not following him. He, then, turned and walked away. Later that evening, the SP's picked him up and booked him for stealing the pistol from his ship.

Honorably Discharged from the U.S. Navy

On October 15th, 1945, I was transferred to the Navy base at Swan Island, which was a short distance from Portland, Oregon. Due to my sea duty time in the war zone, I had enough points to receive my discharge. We would check the roster every morning and evening to see if our name was on the list, and if not, then, we were free to go on liberty or do whatever we desired.

After two weeks, on the morning of November 1st, 1945, my name along with several others was on the roster advising us that we would be catching a train that evening. Our destination would be the Navy Base in Charleston, South Carolina, where I would receive my honorable discharge and be mustered out of the United States Navy. With quite a layover in Chicago, Illinois, we arrived in Charleston on November 6th, 1945. We stayed at the Charleston Navy Base for one week getting our physical and other requirements. On receiving our discharge certificate on November 13th, 1945, we were admonished that we were still in the U.S. Navy for twenty-four hours.

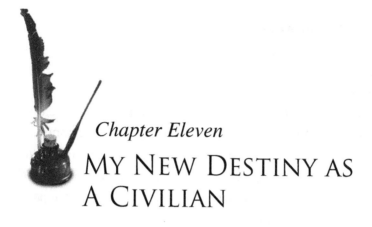

Chapter Eleven
MY NEW DESTINY AS A CIVILIAN

It was good to be home again and to be able to spend time with my new found friend, Frances. Lewis was home, also, and was becoming quite serious with Frankie, and she was becoming quite serious with him. Frances had gone to Linville Falls, North Carolina to spend a few days with her parents. Lewis and I drove up to their place on a weekend, and we were able to meet their parents. I was picking up some work here and there, but had nothing stable.

I met a man who owned his own taxicab, and we became friends. He made trips along with other men to Newport News, Virginia to buy used automobiles. One time he asked me to go along and drive an automobile back for him. He had purchased a very nice automobile and wanted to drive it, so I drove his taxicab.

It was raining steady and hard when we left Newport News, and I was the last automobile following along in the group. A school bus had stopped and was unloading children, so I stopped and was watching the bus driver. When I saw a panic expression on his face, I glanced in my rearview mirror. Just as

I did, my taxicab was struck on the right side of my rear bumper by a car traveling approximately fifty miles an hour. There was an embankment, which he hit and, then, flipped back over into my passenger side. I had just enough time to brace for the crash, so I was uninjured. No one was injured in the other car either.

Later, the bus driver vouched for us being the innocent party of the crash. Therefore, the insurance company of the other driver paid for the damage of the taxicab to be repaired. However, we had to spend one night there for temporary repairs before we could travel on home.

I decided to take a few days and visit my uncle and aunt in Charlotte, North Carolina. My sister, Lorene, also used to work in this town at the A&P Bakery. She suggested that I apply for employment with them, which I did and was hired to start immediately. They would schedule me to work most weekends, which was keeping me from seeing Frances. One weekend, when I was supposed to work, I hitchhiked to see her. The superintendent was upset with me, and the next week he informed me that I was one of his best workers, but they were cutting back and, for the time being, he had to lay me off. I never went back.

I returned to Hickory, North Carolina, and Frances and I were able to have more frequent dates. Frances had a cousin by the name of Paul Shell. We went out with him one night along with another cousin by the name of Carver Weatherman. To this day, I don't know how Frances put up with us, because all three of us were drinking alcohol. Paul was driving and started making a left turn, but he turned too soon and headed down the main railroad track. Frances saved our lives, when she yelled at Paul to stop. He did stop and backed off the track. Moments later, a train came barreling through.

Frances and I had discussed marriage, but we were both hesitant, because I was having problems getting adjusted back to civilian life. I truly loved her, and knew she had to care an awful lot for me or she would not have put up with my indulging too much in beer.

The battle at Okinawa paid a real toll on my life. My nerves were shattered. At night, I would have a bad dream or nightmare. I would see terrible creatures chasing me. I would be running with all my might until I was completely exhausted. My heart felt like it was going to jump out of my chest. Just as these creatures would reach out to grab me, I would somehow go sailing through the air and escape them. I did not want to drink any alcoholic beverage, but it gave me relief for a while. I really wanted Frances for my wife, and we agreed to get married.

Ralph and Frances Getting Serious

Wedding Bells Ring

Frances and I decided to get married on May 21st, 1946. We traveled to Gaffney, South Carolina to a Justice of the Peace and found out that we would have to wait twenty-four hours after applying for our license. We got a couple of rooms at a boarding house with a very nice lady for the night, and the next day on May 22nd, 1946 at 3:00 PM, we were joined in holy matrimony.

As time would testify, our marriage not only made me a happy man, but a very blessed man. I don't know of anyone else that could have done for me and to me what Frances was able to do. Although she was tried severely, she was patient and exercised faith that touched God.

Lewis and Frankie were married on May 2nd, 1946. Frances and I moved to Charlotte, North Carolina and lived with my dad's sister and family for a short period of time. My father-in-law helped us borrow enough money to make it possible for us to purchase a small house trailer. We moved it to a trailer park on North Tryon Street in Charlotte. We did not have any dishes or silverware, so we went to a salvage store and purchased two plates, two forks, two teaspoons, two case knives and two Navy tablespoons. These items were only ten cents each. We also had to purchase a couple of bowls, cups and glasses. We did not have any pillows, but my mother-in-law packed up two pillows and several other items including an electric fan and mailed them to us.

Having a strong interest in sign painting, I went to work for a sign painter by the name of W.R. Grady. All my work here consisted of background painting only and erecting signs, which no skill was needed for that. Then, I left Mr. Grady and went to work for another sign painter. All my work at this place just involved repainting signs on buildings and so on. That job did not pan out either. Meanwhile, my wife had gone to work for a large trucking company as a file clerk.

I decided I would go back into welding. A lady that my wife worked with told her husband that I was looking for work as a welder. He worked for the Southeastern Steel Company and suggested that I check them out for employment. So, the next day I was able to speak with the owner, and he said, *"Can you weld?"* And I replied, *"Yes, sir!"* He said, *"You want to go to work now?"* I explained that I would be there the next morning, which I did and enjoyed working with structural steel.

My wife's mother became quite ill and had to have serious surgery. She was confined to her bed after returning home. We decided that my wife should go home and be with her mother. I remained in Charlotte, North Carolina until a call came informing me that I should travel to my in-laws, because my mother-in-law was not expected to live. Prior to my arrival, she went into a coma, and a few days later passed away on May 8th, 1947 at the age of forty.

My wife and I thought it would be best for us to remain with her father for a while. He had a service (gasoline) station and grocery store, which I helped to operate. A couple of months later, my father-in-law had an oil company to build another station less than a mile from his present station. When this new station was completed, I took it over to operate. My station was just prior to entering the Blue Ridge Parkway, and my father-in law's station was just past the entrance to this Parkway; therefore, we caught the traffic traveling each way.

Our First Child is Born

My wife was pregnant at this time, and on January 1st, 1948 at approximately 4:00 AM, she began having heavy pain, and we knew it was time for our child to be born. We lived in Linville Falls located in the mountains of western North Carolina, which was twenty three miles from the hospital. I did not own an automobile, but a neighbor boy was in the habit of leaving his car at my station, because there was no road to drive it to his house. He had left the keys to his car with me and informed me that if I needed his automobile for any reason, to feel free to use it. This was a real blessing to us on this night.

My mother was visiting with us, and she helped me get my wife ready to go in that car to the hospital. It was raining, and when we started down that mountain, it was so foggy that I had to roll my car window down and watch the white line on the road in order to see where I was going. At 9:40 in the morning, a son was born to us at the General Hospital in Marion, North Carolina. We named him Terry Blaine. While my wife was still in the hospital, I sold out the business, and we moved back to Hickory, North Carolina.

We Purchased Our House

We bought a new house under the G.I. Bill that was located next door to Lewis and Frankie, and I was able to work for the contractor that built the house. He found out that I was a welder and stated that he knew the owners of the Hickory Steel and Iron Company. He offered to go with me to check out employment. After our introduction and a short conversation, the owner instructed me to report the next morning at 7:00 AM.

My nerves were very bad, and I began drinking more and more alcoholic beverages each week. I was working, but spending money foolishly that I certainly could not afford, which was hurting my family. My wife loved me, and I loved her. Many times I would try to resist drinking, but I always failed.

Terry's First Communion Service

In the summer of 1950, we attended the local Baptist church, and they served communion to all that desired to partake. The sanctuary was so quiet that you could hear a pin fall on the carpet. The ushers passed the bread tray very slowly in front of everyone. As it was passing by us, our two-and-a-half-year-old son, Terry, grabbed a handful of bread, slapped it into his mouth and yelled out very loudly, *"More bread, Mommy. More bread!"* I am sure that everyone in the sanctuary heard him, and I had to grab him and exit the church.

Our Second Child is Born

On December 15th, 1950 at 12:10 AM, Terry, who was now only two weeks away from age three, woke me up out of a sound sleep and said, *"Daddy, mommy is sick."* I jumped up out of bed, and she said, *"I think it is time for our child to be born."* I grabbed my son and took him to our neighbor's house for her to watch him, while I hurriedly drove to the hospital, arriving at 12:40 AM. In a few minutes, I saw our doctor running down the hall, and twenty minutes after we arrived at the hospital, our daughter, Karen, was born at 1:00 AM in the Memorial Hospital of Hickory, North Carolina. The doctor came out and said, *"Why didn't you get your wife here sooner?"* I said, *"Doctor, if I had not heard my son when he called me, I would not have arrived at the hospital in time."*

Chapter Twelve

UNITED WE STAND, DIVIDED WE FALL

Korean War

In 1950, the year our daughter was born, America went to war with North Korea. This war continued until 1953. This was a terrible war. The American Battle Commission Database for the Korean War gives the following report of the Department of Defense, which states that "During the Korean War, 54,246 American service men and women lost their lives plus thousands more were wounded."

Defense Work Again

When the United States entered war against North Korea, I felt that it was my patriotic duty to seek work in a defense plant. After working for the Hickory Steel and Iron Company for three years, I left that job in good standing and decided to travel to Baltimore, Maryland where my brother lived. My purpose for relocating to Baltimore was to seek employment in the shipyard or aircraft factory.

Early on Sunday morning, March 4th, 1951, I left on my journey and arrived at my destination late in the afternoon. On Monday, I went to the employment office at the shipyard and was sent to take a welding test. I passed the test and was scheduled to start work on Wednesday. However, on Monday evening, I went to the employment office at the Glen L. Martin Aircraft Company. I was interviewed and went back on Tuesday to take the welding test for employment there. It was late in the afternoon when I finished my welding test and physical, which I passed both of them. Due to the lateness of the evening, I had to wait until Thursday, March 8th, 1951, to begin work. I decided this was a much better place to work, so I chose it over the shipyard.

Vietnam War

In the 1960's, the United States got involved in the war defending South Vietnam against North Vietnam. In this Vietnam War, there were 500,000 United States Troops involved at one time. There were over 59,000 American lives lost and a great number of troops wounded. This war was altogether different from World War Two. Many of the American citizens opposed this war, and thousands gathered at the Pentagon and other places to protest this war. Many people were disrespectful to our troops. What a lot of people do not realize is the fact that when a person is sworn into military service, the government owns that person. Troops have to obey the orders of their superiors.

Mideast Wars

In more recent years, we have been involved (and are at this very moment) in major conflicts with Iraq, Iran, Afghanistan and other countries. All of these battles that I have listed have all taken place in my lifetime, but the greatest battle yet to be fought is not too far in the future. It may still take place while I am still alive on this earth. It is closer than many of us can even realize.

A United America

The true reason we Americans were able to come from behind and excel in World War Two was because everyone was on the same page. Back then, the whole nation of the United States of America was in unity at war against the enemy. There is tremendous power in unity. Young men were called upon to bear arms while the older men filled the defense factories along with women. There was "Rosie the Riveter," women welders, and many other positions filled by volunteers. A great unified desire swept over our nation that caused us to excel. Our culture today in our beloved America is a long way from the patriotism that was known during World War Two and prior years.

When World War Two ended, there was a feeling for many that this was the war of wars that would end all wars. However, we are in for a great awakening. The Battle of Armageddon and World War Three will surely take place. The Scripture found in the book of Revelation chapter nine tells us that one-third of mankind on the earth shall die. The population today on earth is over seven billion people. The Bible is true prophecy from God warning the population of this world. It plainly states that at the end of the world, *"There shall be wars and rumors of wars"* (Matthew 24:6–8 KJV). It goes on to inform us that *"One generation passes and another generation comes"* (Ecclesiastes 1:4 KJV). People will always be people, some morally good and others quite wicked.

"In God We Trust" is America's national motto. There are those who know nothing about this nation's beginning and her struggle for survival. They think this motto is some Christian or right-wing political slogan. Every American should be aware that this motto was adopted, because Christian men and women founded this nation on Biblical principles, which is clearly documented in the annals of American history. America has her own multi–ethnic Christian culture, and the idea of incorporating non–Christian cultures into her governmental laws would only serve to dilute her and cause her to lose her sovereignty and national identity. The development of our culture has come about over centuries of struggles, trials and victories by millions of men and women who have sought the freedom we enjoy with many that paid the supreme price to preserve America.

"The Father of Our Constitution" made the following statement: *"We have staked the whole of all our political institutions upon the capacity of mankind for self-government, upon the capacity of each and all of us to govern ourselves, to control ourselves, to sustain ourselves according to the Ten Commandments of God."* People today should backpedal to the beginning of this nation, where America's very first Supreme Court Judge, John Jay, said: *"Americans should select and prefer Christians as their rulers."*

The politically, educationally and judicially correct crowd complains about the possibility of our patriotism to our nation being offensive to others. Our mother tongue is English and not Spanish or any other language. Anyone wishing to become part of our society needs to learn the English language just as our ancestors did when they arrived at Ellis Island from Germany, Poland and other European non-English speaking countries. In fact, in order to become naturalized citizens, it is my opinion that such persons should be required to learn English before being granted U.S. citizenship.

America is the land of the free and the home of the brave. Anyone that settles in this wonderful nation should be thankful for the privilege of being permitted to do so. These people have no right to come whining and griping about our flag, our pledge or our national motto.

I love America. I have fought for her freedom, and I have seen men die to preserve her freedom. We believe in the true almighty God. If that offends anyone, there is another great American freedom, which is the right to relocate somewhere else in the universe. People of all persuasions have the right, privilege and freedom in America to follow any religious beliefs they desire. Nevertheless, everyone needs to understand that America is a Christian nation that was founded upon Biblical principles. There are some people that have tried to overthrow what America has stood for over the years and have succeeded to a certain extent.

America has gradually drifted away from Godly principles and beliefs until today she is not even recognized as the nation she used to be. I pray to God that everyone who still holds on to righteousness and truth would stand up, band together and take back America. The Scripture states, *"If my people, which are called by my name, shall humble themselves, and pray, and seek my face, and turn from their wicked ways; then will I hear from heaven, and will forgive their sin, and will heal their land"* (II Chronicles 7:14 KJV).

God has richly blessed this nation, but more and more with each passing day, our educators, judges and elected political leaders are determined to please rabble-rousers and push God completely out of the picture. Some of these people are working hard to make it illegal to pray or preach in the name of Jesus.

When you do away with God, you lose your protection. It is high time for us to pray for America, because she is on a free fall to her destruction. The people need to wake up and realize that the Bible is the Word of God, and it states in Psalm 9:17 (KJV), *"The wicked shall be turned into hell, and **ALL THE NATIONS** (emphasis mine) that forget God."* Thank God for true Christian patriots! They are the heart and soul of America.

Cultural Changes in America

It is not only disheartening, but heartbreaking when we see and hear of the disrespect for authority from many people for our elected leadership of today. We realize that we are in trouble. The leaders of our beloved United States of America are in a political warfare.

I read of some remarks coming out of Hollywood stating that they are ashamed they are Americans due to the war in Iraq. It was a much different story during World War Two. Movie stars, professional athletes and many others immediately enlisted in the armed services, because they knew their nation was in trouble and needed them. Some of these folks were awarded medals for outstanding performance, some of them were wounded in battle and some of them paid the supreme price of giving their lives for their country.

In the past, we (as Americans) did not go to the aid of certain foreign countries and risk our lives in wars to defend their freedoms in order for them, decades later, to come over here to America and try to convince us that our Constitution is a living document that is open to their interpretations. My friends and buddies didn't die in vain, so people could leave their native birth countries to come over here and disrespect our wonderful country.

In our beloved America, it is sickening today when we see these statements of "Political Correctness." I am acquainted with many wonderful black people, and not a half-dozen of them were born in Africa. They are American born. So, how can they be "African-Americans?" Africa is a continent. <u>They are Americans as much as I am American!</u>

I don't go around saying I am a European–American, because my great, great, great, great, great grandfather immigrated from Europe. I was born in America and proud to be from America. <u>I am an American!</u> Period! I proudly stand for the playing and singing of our National Anthem and honor our American flag and great Republic. The Pledge of Allegiance stated below means more to me than just recited words. It represents enormous sacrifice to preserve the liberties we enjoy.

"I PLEDGE ALLEGIANCE TO THE FLAG, OF THE UNITED STATES OF AMERICA, AND TO THE REPUBLIC, FOR WHICH IT STANDS, ONE NATION <u>UNDER GOD</u>, INDIVISIBLE, WITH LIBERTY AND JUSTICE FOR ALL!"

In the beginning our nation was formed by men and women who believed in Almighty God and confessed the Lord Jesus Christ as their Savior. They all professed to be Christians. They were genuine in what they believed. I read in a document of a survey taken that the largest majority today of American citizens profess to be Christians. They claim to love the Lord, but the sad fact is that many of them don't even know the Lord. Jesus said, *"If you love me, you will keep my commandments"* (John 14:15 KJV). There are so many professors, but few possessors.

In order to love the Lord, you must be born again as recorded in Acts 2:38-39. These Scriptures state, *"Then Peter said, Repent and be baptized, every one of you, in the name of Jesus Christ for the remission of sins, and you shall receive the gift of the Holy Ghost. For the promise is unto you, and to your children, and to all that are afar off, even as many as the Lord our God shall call."* The voice of Peter was the voice of God speaking through Peter. This is the birth of the church which Jesus is building!

Therefore, with all of these people confessing to be Christians, I have a very hard time understanding why there is such a problem in having *"In God We Trust"* on our currency and having *"Under God"* in the Pledge of Allegiance. It is time that blue–blooded Americans, real patriots, stand up and tell those that are rising up against everything that is rooted and grounded in the foundation that has made America great to *"Sit down and Be Quiet!"*

Patrick Henry, a Patriot and Founding Father of our country, said, *"It cannot be emphasized too strongly or too often that this great nation was founded not by religionists, but by Christians, not on religions, but on the Gospel of Jesus Christ."* Psalm 11-3 (KJV) states *"If the foundations be destroyed, what can the righteous do?"*

America, over the years, has been on a downward slide a little at a time. Since the beginning of my days on this earth in the 1920's, those days are hard to recognize in any form today. People used to be God-conscious and strove to be honest before God in their daily life. They had a heart of compassion for their fellow man.

Today, many of our elected political leaders, judges and educators have determined to push God completely out of the picture. They take an oath on the Word of God to consciously be for the people, but knowing in their heart that they have no intention of carrying out that oath. These people do not have this nation or the people at heart. They are power hungry and go to all extent to satisfy their personal greed. They look at themselves as leaders, but they refuse to follow a leader.

There are those working hard to pass laws called hate crimes for ministers of the gospel to preach against certain lifestyles that the Word of God condemns. This is a tremendous difference than what it was in my days of youth. During those days, people operated in the fear of God.

Today, these people are doing evil, because they are inspired by Satan, the god of this world. The true God is light, and in Him is no darkness. I used to be spiritually blind, but God rescued me, opened my blinded eyes and shone His glorious light into my life.

If we are Christians today, we should never be ashamed to let the world know whose side we are on. Today, wrong signs are displayed everywhere. Many of America's top selling books are angry, in-your-face and atheistic manifestos. Judges try to outdo each other in banning from schools and government places references to God, such as prayer, the Ten Commandments and so on.

According to statistics presently compiled, many Americans are infatuated with outright, full-blown atheism. Somehow, atheism just like homosexuality, which used to be considered shameful and something to hide, is now becoming hip, enlightened, sophisticated and even a badge of honor.

How can this be happening, you might wonder? Do you really want to know the truth? The truth lies in the fact that many people have turned their backs on God. They do not have time for God; therefore, Satan is taking over. Without God we are no match against the devil.

In our nation, there was a time when many people had a belief in God and a place of worship in which they were devout and faithful to every week. However, if you check the statistics today, you will find many people in this generation have dropped out of their Christian faith in droves, giving up completely on God.

In most every home in America, there is probably at least one or more copies of the "Holy Bible." Yet, it is the most neglected book of all. If you want the Lord, you must seek Him through His Word and through sincere prayer while He can be found. Your prayer needs to be, *"Open my spiritual eyes, Lord, because I want to see you clearly."* America needs a spiritual renewal.

As previously stated, America was founded on Christian principles. Her very purpose for being was religious freedom and the furtherance of Biblical Christianity according to the Pilgrims and succeeding generations. The nation's school system was created for the express purpose of propagating the Christian faith. The first schools were in churches, the first teachers were pastors and the first textbook was the Bible. Almost all of the Founding Fathers who drafted and signed the Constitution were Christian believers.

Revelation 12:12 (NIV) states, *"Therefore rejoice, you heavens and you who dwell in them! But woe to the earth and the sea, because the devil has gone down to you! He is filled with fury, because he knows that his time is short."* Satan has people blinded!

William Booth stated, *"The chief danger of the 20th century will be religion without the Holy Ghost, Christianity without Christ, forgiveness without repentance, salvation without regeneration, politics without God, and Heaven without Hell."*

There are many religions today, but the Holy Ghost is not present. Many people claim to be Christians, but they do not have Christ. To be a child of God, you must receive the baptism of the Holy Ghost and bear His name. Search the Scriptures and you will find that every one that was baptized with the Holy Spirit spoke in another tongue or language that they did not know. Romans 8:9 (KJV) informs us, *"But ye are not in the flesh, but in the Spirit, if so be that the Spirit of God dwell in you. Now if any man have not the Spirit of Christ, he is none of His."*

Chapter Thirteen

THE DIFFERENCE JESUS MAKES

M y mother, a widow for a number of years, had married Doctor W.S. Watson, a foot culturist. His office was on a main street in Hickory, North Carolina. On a particular day before my conversion, after having a few beers, I was passing by his office when he stepped out onto the street. When he saw that I had indulged, he said, *"You ought to be ashamed."*

If he had only known the turmoil in which I was going through with my shattered nerves, maybe, he would have been more sympathetic. I, also, knew that if there had been any love, it was lost during that moment. Thankfully, it was temporary anger, and I did forgive him, because I knew he was thinking of the hurt it caused my mother.

One time his own brother, whom he had not seen in several years, came by to see him after having a few drinks. Doctor Watson told him to leave, and that he never wanted to see him again. His brother saw to it that his wishes were carried out.

Doctor Watson was a devout political party man on the Republican side. I was never a political party man, but when I was around Doctor Watson, I immediately became a strong

Democrat. It was a delight for me to argue with him and get a rise out of him.

However, things changed in my attitude towards him after my conversion. Sometime after I had given my heart to the Lord, we made a trip to Hickory, North Carolina to visit my mother. Doctor Watson noticed the change in my life and made a comment to my mother, *"I don't know what Ralph has got, but it is for keeps."* Doctor Watson was a good moral man, and he was good for my mother. They got along very well, and for this I highly respected him.

Answers to my Youthful Questions

Years later, after my new birth conversion, I began to receive answers to things that had me mystified. I learned that God was a Spirit, and the Holy Bible was His Word; therefore, it was a "Spiritual book." Romans 8:7 (KJV) tells us, *"Because the carnal mind is enmity against God: for it is not subject to the law (word) of God, neither indeed can be."* The carnal mind is without understanding of the Spiritual. When God baptizes us with His Holy Spirit as recorded in the book of Colossians, it becomes *"Christ in you, the hope of glory"* (Colossians 1:27 KJV).

When I began my search of the Scriptures, I found the answers to my youthful pondering. I found in Psalms 147:4 that *"He tells the number of the stars; he calleth them all by their names."* I knew that if God knew the names of every star, He certainly knew my name. The Holy Bible is God's Word. It is the most astounding literature book ever written and is as fresh as tomorrow's newspaper.

I soon came to the realization that our family had survived the heartaches and struggles, in which we had faced and endured, due to the mercy of God. In seemingly all appearance, there was no way that we could survive, but I came to the knowledge that there is nothing impossible with God. The Scriptures enlightened me to the fact that God's mercy reaches out to all people, but it's when we, as individuals, reach out to Him that we find grace. It is His grace that saves us when we seek Him.

As for me, the more I learn about Jesus and the longer I walk with Him, the greater my desire becomes to spend an eternity with Him. My prayer is, *"Lord, help me to always remember where you brought me from to where I am today."*

Alcohol Addiction

A couple of years prior to my salvation in 1953, we had moved to Baltimore, Maryland from Hickory, North Carolina seeking employment. I was hired at the Glenn L. Martin Aircraft Company. My job at Martin's Aircraft Factory consisted of being a fixture builder. We built the fixtures that aircraft parts, wings, stabilizers, fuselage, etc. were assembled on.

At this time I was having a battle with my nerves and began stopping at the bars and having a few drinks on my way home almost every day. I was working my full week job every week, and my wife was being very patient with me. At times I would be able to go for two or three months without stopping at the bars, and suddenly, my nerves would flare up again, and I would have those frightening dreams. I would begin drinking alcohol again. Gradually, my drinking problem was winning, taking its toll on my life and causing my family to suffer. At the age of twenty-nine, I had become an alcoholic. I was spending money that my family certainly needed. I would try to quit drinking, but my defense was too weak.

My wife's Aunt Lottie, who lived in North Carolina, was a devout saint of God, having been baptized in Jesus' name and having received the baptism of the Holy Ghost. Realizing that our family was very fragile due to my drinking problem, she approached two other Godly ladies from church and enlisted them to join her in fasting and praying for my family and me. After spending eight consecutive days in fasting and prayer for our family, God began to work in miraculous ways.

I worked second shift from 3:00 PM until 11:00 PM. After work on Thursday evening, April 30th, 1953, four of us fellows went to a bar and stayed until closing time at 2:00 AM. When the bar closed, we went to the home of one of these fellows and spent the rest of the night talking and drinking. On Friday morning, May 1st, 1953, after spending Thursday night drinking, I headed home. At this time I did not have the least idea that my wife had planned to take our two children and leave me on this very day.

On the Ledge of Hell

As I was in my automobile and driving home, suddenly, I had a startling vision or an unexplainable experience that was so real. In this experience I was not in my automobile. I was sailing high up through the air. I don't know how long I was traveling through the air when, all of a sudden, I realized that I was not sailing through the air any longer, but I was standing on a ledge. When I looked down, I saw a vast area of a blazing lake of fire with multitudes of people as far as the eye could see. They were running in that fire with no escape, screaming and wailing like I could never imagine. I stood there looking and wondering where I was.

For the first time in my life, I heard the voice of God or I might say that it was the first time I recognized the voice of God speaking to me. He spoke to my spirit and said, *"This is hell!"* I was on the brink of hell! I had not landed into the fire yet. My thoughts were, *"I have heard about this place all of my life, and now I am here!"*

There is no way to explain how I felt. I don't know how long this vision lasted, but the next thing I realized was that I was sailing back through the air and ending up sitting back in my car. Somehow, my car had stopped on the side of the road. I had been highly intoxicated when this vision began, but now I was sober and perspiring. Later in life, I realized that sincere prayer and fasting had saved me from hell.

Looking back into my past, it was easier to see how the Lord was working in my life. It wasn't very obvious at the time. My childhood struggles had actually worked together for good. God's Word states that *"... He has set eternity in the human heart..."* (Ecclesiastes 3:11 NIV). The meaning of this Scripture is that deep in each heart abides a longing for something much greater than what we can find in things that this world can offer.

Although my world began to crumble at an early age, it actually gave me an advantage. Working through the many problems that I faced as a child caused me to focus more on reasons for living. Even though Satan tried in many ways to destroy me, my quest finally led me to a true loving God.

As I look back, I can see how the extended hand of this wonderful Savior has sustained, protected and healed me in His quest of reaching for me. His will for my life directed me to other geographical parts of the world, witnessing various different cultures and participating in a war, which all gave me tremendous insight.

There was a time in my past that Satan had me so completely chained and shackled. I was a spiritual slave and no match with my humanistic effort to combat the hold that the devil had on my life. I was living a life of misery and even contemplated ending it all by taking my life. I was truly at the end of the road.

But, thanks be to my Lord and Savior, Jesus Christ, for His intervention! He is the only true God who knew me even though I did not know Him. On this particular morning, God literally snatched me out of the eternal fires of hell. My desires were completely changed that day. I'm so blessed that God looks on the heart.

I have often wondered why some people become so acutely aware of their great need for God to the point of actually hungering and thirsting after Him while, yet on the other hand, other people seemingly cannot get their ducks in a row enough to even acknowledge that He exists. I really count myself fortunate that Jesus made a believer out of me.

My father-in-law lived with us, and he watched out for our children while my wife worked a job on the day shift. When I came home, I took the children off his hands. On one particular day, I took our children to a neighbor for her to watch them while I ran an errand. My wife arrived home just a few minutes before I did and was really upset when she found the children gone. When I drove up, she met me and was almost hysterical, wanting to know where her children were. I informed her that they were fine and were at our neighbor's house. I said, *"Look, honey, I have got to talk with you."*

At the time I did not explain my vision of hell to her, but I began to tell her how sorry I was for causing her so much worry and heartache. I began to confess my wrongs and told her that I truly loved her. I acknowledged that I knew that it would not be easy, but I hoped she could find it in her heart to forgive me. I stressed to her that I would never drink another alcoholic beverage, and that we must find the church that her Aunt Lottie attended when she visited us in Baltimore. I promised her that we would attend this church regularly. My wife said, *"You have never been a convincing liar, and there is something different about you. Somehow, I partially believe you."*

I am amazed in the way in which the Lord performs in the life of individuals. Approximately one month prior to my vision of hell experience, two Jewish salesmen knocked on my door selling different items or products. I informed them that I was not in the market for anything. One of them said, *"I have something in my car that I believe you would really like."*

He returned to his car and came back with this Bible. It was over two inches thick. When he opened it and started showing me all of these great helps that made the Bible easier to understand, I was ready to say, *"No,"* when he said, *"Look, this Bible is only twenty dollars. I come through here every week. Just give me one dollar each week with no interest."* I agreed. When they left and I realized they had just sold me a Bible of all things, I thought that they could sell snowballs to Eskimos.

We decided to try to find the church that Aunt Lottie attended in Baltimore when she came to visit us. We were told that it was located on "Austin" Street, so we searched for it the next week. We were unable to find this street. We even checked with the police department, but no one there was familiar with a street in Baltimore by that name.

Aunt Lottie, not knowing what had taken place in our home, felt the Lord dealing with her to pay us another visit. So, she boarded a bus and traveled to our home in Baltimore. There was a knock on our door. When I opened the door and saw her standing there, I said, *"Aunt Lottie, it is good to see you, but what brings you here all the way from North Carolina?"* She said, *"I don't know, but I was praying and the Lord spoke to my heart to go to Baltimore, so here I am."* I said, *"I may know why you are here—we have searched for that church that you attended and could not find it. Do you know the address?"*

She said, *"No, I do not know the address. But, I rode the bus and remember the way the driver went. I can show you where it is if you follow the bus route."*

We decided to attend the Saturday evening service on May 16th, 1953. Aunt Lottie gave good directions. When we arrived at the church, we found out that the name of the street that the church was on was "Ostend" and not "Austin."

Aunt Lottie was raised on a small farm in western North Carolina. She never attended enough school to learn to read or write, and she regularly attended services at a denominational church. After meeting with some Pentecostal people and seeing their love and worship of God, she pondered it all in her heart.

At the farm, in the orchard, she knelt under an apple tree and began to pray. Her prayer was *"Lord, you know my heart, and I want everything you have for me."* After a period of prayer, the Spirit of the Lord came upon her. She jumped to her feet, and began to dance and speak in tongues just like the hundred and twenty disciples did that had gathered in the upper room in Jerusalem as recorded in the second chapter of the book of Acts. A short time later, baptism in Jesus' name was revealed to her, and she was baptized in that wonderful name.

Aunt Lottie had the pure faith of a child, and she wanted to be able to read the Bible. So, she prayed unto the Lord asking Him to help her to read and understand the Scriptures. God heard and answered her prayer in an amazing way. God enabled her with the ability to pick up the Bible and read it word for word. However, she could not read a newspaper or any other written material. When she corresponded with our family, she had to get someone else to write for her, and when we wrote to her, she had to have someone else read it to her.

There were several times when I asked Aunt Lottie to pray for some prayer requests. She would tell me, *"Don't you doubt, for the work is already done."* Almost before the words were out of her mouth, the prayers were answered.

On one occasion, I really had a hard time not doubting, but to my amazement, in a very short time, this prayer was also answered. I began to see that God's great anointing was upon her life, and her prayers were highly effective.

It is amazing grace that Aunt Lottie would take up a burden for me and would even enlist a couple of her church friends to call upon the Lord on my behalf. Before I really knew her, I thought she was a little wacky. I mistook her spirituality for fanaticism and gave her a hard time, but to be truthful, I was afraid of her.

I had told her once that if what she and her church had was real, I wanted it; but, if it was not real, they should get the hottest place in Hell. After my conversion, I asked her how she ever tolerated me. She said, *"Many times I covered my head with a pillow and cried out to the Lord to save you."* That truly humbled me.

True Repentance

This church on Ostend Street was in a store front building. The first time we nervously entered the doors of this building to attend this church we were met by a nice group of very friendly people. The service began with a piano, guitar and a couple of tambourines. The people sang heartily in worship with hands raised, and several of them began to dance.

I felt miserable through the song service and worse through the preaching. I don't remember the title of the message the pastor preached that night, but I felt that the message was just straight to me.

When the invitation was given for all to come forward and pray, I wanted to go forward, but it felt as though my feet were glued to the floor. An appealing song was being sung, and I told myself that we would return the next day, which was Sunday, and I would go forward, then.

However, the convicting power of God was dealing so strongly with me that, suddenly, the next thing I realized was the fact that I had ended up on my knees at the altar with people praying for me. To this day, I don't remember moving out of my seat or have any idea how I arrived at that altar, but I found myself repenting of my sins and crying out to God.

Water Baptism

After my first experience at the altar, my feet became unglued, and it was easier to go forward and pray. We attended four services each week unless there was a revival, in which we would attend every night.

After attending this church for two weeks, on May 30th, a brother spoke to me about baptism, and I said, *"I have a smoking problem, and I feel I have to get rid of that habit before baptism."* His reply was, *"Get baptized and the Lord will deliver you."*

But, I felt to truly repent I had to lay aside my cigarettes. At the altar that night, I told the Lord that if He gave me the strength to overcome, I would die before I would smoke another cigarette.

When we left church, I told Aunt Lottie to get my full pack of Camels (cigarettes) out of the glove compartment and toss them out the car window. She said, *"Brother, I wish you meant that, because I have seen you throw them away before, and then, go out and buy more."* I said, *"Do it! Things will be different this time."* She did as I requested, and I will never forget seeing that full pack of Camels through my rearview mirror, lying in the middle of Light Street in South Baltimore, where the famous Baltimore Inner Harbor is now located.

The devil fought me in a great way of temptation. Six months later, I had a vivid dream that I was smoking again. That dream was so real that I thought, *"After all this time I have held out, and now I have blown it!"* When I awoke and realized it was a dream, I had the pleasure and privilege to shout in the devil's face, *"Satan, it didn't work!"* I gave thanks to God who gave me the strength to resist and hold out.

On Saturday night I asked the pastor if my wife and I could be baptized the next day. So, on June 7th, 1953, we were both baptized in water by immersion in the name of Jesus Christ. This took place in the Chesapeake Bay near the Hanover Street bridge in South Baltimore.

When we arrived home that evening, I explained to my wife and Aunt Lottie the vision I had concerning the lake of fire, which was the turning point in my life that led to my repentance and conversion. Aunt Lottie spoke up and said, *"Brother, I put you on the prayer list at church and two farmer ladies and I fasted and prayed for your family for eight days."*

These ladies worked in the field, prepared meals for their families and fasted for us —people they did not know. Their fast ended on the day that I had the vision of being on the brink of hell. Thank God for people who, with a sincere burden, can touch the heavenly throne in prayers of concern.

God put a great desire and hunger in my heart to read and study the Word of God. He, also, put a strong desire in my heart to listen to gospel music and songs. When I would come home from work, I would put on some gospel music and read my Bible awhile before eating dinner.

The new Bible I had bought from those Jewish salesmen was ideal. I don't know how I would have made it spiritually without having that Bible. I did not have a mentor nor anyone else that I could call upon for help in my studies. I knew nothing about Apostolic Bible Colleges. Flesh and blood did not reveal the truth of God's Word to me. It was the Lord that opened my spiritually blinded eyes. I prayed and searched the Bible, and God began to open my understanding to the Scriptures.

I had tried some religions with different denominations, but I knew some leaders in those churches that did not live a life very much different from the sinful life that I lived. They smoked, drank beer and told ungodly jokes.

In my studies of church history, I learned that in the Reformation of the sixteenth century when people broke away from the Roman Catholic Church, they still held on to the Catholic doctrine of baptism in the <u>titles</u> of Father, Son and Holy Ghost instead of following the Scriptures and baptizing converts in the <u>name</u> of the Father, Son and Holy Ghost, which is Jesus Christ.

Anyone that is sincere concerning his or her soul's salvation needs to take time and study the history as recorded in the Bible and documented in different encyclopedias and reference books. All of these reference books and historical study guides plainly document that from the birth of the early church in 33 A.D. until the third century, the only water baptism practiced by the church was by immersion in the name of Jesus Christ for the remission of sins.

It takes Calvary's shed blood to remit sins, and that blood is in the name of Jesus. Acts 4:12 (KJV) declares, *"Neither is there salvation in any other: for there is none other name under heaven given among men, whereby we must be saved."* Anyone who preaches any other doctrine is not preaching the truth, but is preaching a "man–made" dogma. I want to go to heaven, and I want you to go to heaven. Please believe me, this is the only way to be saved. To deny this truth is to be eternally lost. Only obedience to the truth can save you.

We attended all of the weekly services at church and were thrilled when there was a revival where we could go every night. We did not miss our opportunities to seek for the baptism of the Holy Ghost. But, with all of our praying, it seemed as though we just could not break through to the throne of grace.

We would fast and pray and search our lives as to why we were not being baptized with the Holy Spirit. I even wondered if I had blasphemed against God in some manner, and therefore, could not receive this wonderful gift from God. In prayer, the Spirit of God would quicken my body, but I, for some reason, could not receive the baptism of the Holy Spirit.

Baptism of the Holy Spirit

On a Saturday evening, October 3rd, 1953, my wife and I had been praying for some time at the altar with brothers and sisters praying with us. God saw the hunger and desire in our hearts. I heard Aunt Lottie say, *"She's got the Holy Ghost!"* I knew that "she" was my wife, and I said, *"Lord, I know that You have filled my wife with your Spirit, and You know that she cannot live with me and keep the victory of the Holy Spirit unless You baptize me also. And, Lord, if You don't fill me with your Spirit, I intend to be here when the sun rises in the morning."*

Believe me, as the time approached midnight, I thought, maybe, that was really going to happen. I became worn out from praying so hard. Then, there appeared a transparent form just above me. I reached up a little higher, and my fingers touched the form. While still on my knees, I stretched up as far as I could, and that form seemed to drop inside of me, as I began to speak in an unknown tongue like they did in the upper room in Jerusalem as recorded in the second chapter of the book of Acts.

Our wait to receive the baptism of the Holy Spirit was truly a blessing in disguise. God knew our hearts and how hungry and sincere we were to receive the Holy Spirit. That waiting period through extended prayer strengthened us and built our faith in Him.

I am ever thankful for a wife that readily surrendered her life to the Lord in repentance the same night that I did. We were both baptized together in water in Jesus' name the same day, and we both received the Holy Ghost on the same night. We became new creatures in Christ.

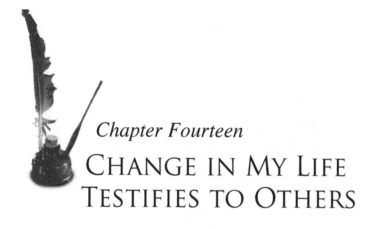

Chapter Fourteen

CHANGE IN MY LIFE
TESTIFIES TO OTHERS

M y next door neighbor, Kenneth Arnett, and I used to go out to the bars together drinking, but when I gave my heart to the Lord, Kenneth said to my son, *"Terry, in all my life, I have never seen the change in any life like that which happened to your dad. One night Ralph was out drinking, and a few nights later he was completely changed and going to church with a Bible under his arm."* Many thanks unto the Lord for a salvation that can be readily recognized!

On the job, a fellow worker by the name of Bucky Boyce and I were very good friends. He was telling everyone that he could tell that I had become a Christian. Different ones brought fixture parts into our welding booth to have us to weld them.

One day, this Italian worker brought a part in for me to weld, and he said, *"Mac, I understand that you got religion."* I informed him that I had surrendered my life to the Lord. He said, *"They, also, tell me that you have given up smoking."* I said, *"Yes, that is true."* He took a long drag on a cigarette and blew the smoke in my face, and said, *"Don't that taste good?"* I still did not know a lot of Scripture, but a quote from the Bible that the pastor had used popped into my mind, and I said, *"Get thee behind me, Satan."* His face turned red, but he left my booth and never bothered me again.

Ralph, Frances, Karen & Terry – Easter 1955

Faith Tested

The fellows that I worked with knew my life, because we had gone out to the bars together. I had been out on the floor working a welding job, and when I returned to our welding booth, there were several of the fellows laying out money on the table. I said, *"What's going on here with this money deal?"* They said, *"Mac, we are betting that your religion doesn't last six months."* I said, *"Fellas, you are going to lose. I didn't get religion. I got salvation, and it is for keeps."* They sure tried hard to discourage me, but thank God for the part of Scripture that I later learned in 1 John 4:4, *"Greater is He that is in you, than he that is in the world."*

Later, I found out that they were speaking well to others about my conversion. When our general foreman came by to wish me a "Merry Christmas," he said, *"Mac, the fellas are telling me that you used to be a real rounder, but you have been converted. They believe that you are now a genuine Christian, because you surely are not the fellow you used to be."* I said, *"Yes sir! I surrendered my life to the Lord, and now I am walking a different path."*

News of my conversion began to spread throughout the plant where I worked, and fellow workers from different denominational beliefs began to come around and talk with me. When I explained that I was traveling eleven miles one way to church, they would exclaim that there was no need to drive that distance, and they invited me to join them in their place of worship. One fellow tried extremely hard and was quite persistent that I would attend church with him. However, I refused all their requests, because I knew beyond the shadow of doubt that I was where the Lord wanted me to be.

I thought that it was strange that I had worked with these same people for two years without any one of them ever mentioning the Lord to me or inviting me to worship with them until I surrendered my life to the Lord. I knew this was Satan working through them to try to get me so discouraged and disgusted that I would quit, and go back to my old life.

I am very thankful now that they did not approach me sooner, because I eventually found out that all of these people believed in the doctrine of the Trinity with baptism in the "titles" rather than the "name" of Jesus. It is very possible that if I had been approached by them and consented to join with them, I would have never come into the enlightenment of the

"Apostolic Faith." God is building only one church, which is a church that bears His name. This one true church is open for all people.

Regaining Wife's Confidence

With the new birth of water and the Spirit experience for both of us, it took my wife quite some time to really relax and believe that it was for keeps. If I ran thirty minutes or so late, she began to get very nervous.

One Sunday evening I parked our car on the street under a large tree while attending church. It happened to be a roosting place for a large flock of birds. When we came out of service, our car was such a mess. I had to clean the windshield before we could drive home. The next day, on my way home from work, I stopped at a service station and washed my car, which took about an hour.

When I arrived home, my wife was really glad to see me; but, later she told me she had done some extra praying. She was afraid that I had slipped back into my old lifestyle, because since my conversion, I had never run that late coming home. However, when God truly changes a person, that person become a completely new creature. Old things pass away and all things become new.

Deceived into Leaving Our Mother Church

The Church of the Lord Jesus Christ, where we received our new birth experience, was a body of very friendly people that truly worshiped God. It is amazing how a person will pick out certain people and build their confidence so strongly in them. We became very close friends with this man and his wife, because they seemed to be extra spiritual.

When a problem arose in the church, this couple persuaded my wife and me to leave and help them start another church. Thinking it was the will of God, we consented and helped them find another storefront building to rent. The Lord was merciful to us in our ignorance. Although we did have some good services for a while, it didn't last. The newness of this adventure began to wear off, and my wife and I began to feel uncomfortable. We shared our feelings with this couple, and they told us that it was just the devil trying to break us up.

Finally, I called the pastor where we had been saved and invited him and his wife to visit us. They came to our home, were very friendly and never once scolded us for leaving the church. After visiting with them for a while, we told them that we would like to come back to their church. They were thrilled that we were returning home and made us feel very welcome in the congregation.

Blessings Received After Returning to Our Spiritual Home

One day my wife started breaking out in a rash and swelling throughout her body. In fact, her eyes had almost swollen shut. We prayed for the situation and the rash went away along with the swelling.

My wife's Aunt Lottie paid us another visit, and we went to church on Saturday evening. Shortly after we arrived home, my wife began to break out in a heavy rash and swelling again. Aunt Lottie said, *"Brother, let's pray."* After praying for a while, we stopped, and I confess that it seemed as though my prayers were up against a wall. Aunt Lottie said, *"Brother, let's pray again."*

In a little bit, a family from the church knocked on the door and said that the Lord had led them to our house. A few minutes later a second family from the church came to our house. Before it was over, two more families from the church showed up at our home. None of the four families knew the others were coming, but each of them said that the Lord led them to our house. They joined with us in prayer for my wife.

After we had prayed a short while, it felt like all heaven opened up in our living room. My wife rose up from where she was sitting and began to dance and shout. I could see the rash fading and the swelling leaving her body.

The next morning when my wife awoke, she began to look at her arms and feel her face. I said, *"Don't look for it, because it is gone."* She never had another problem with that again, and to this moment we never did know what had plagued her.

About 1:00 AM one morning, our three-year-old daughter entered our bedroom. She was crying and holding her side saying, *"It hurts."* I reached out and lifted her onto the bed between my wife and me. We began to pray and shortly she said, *"It quit hurting."* I had her stay in the bed with us for the rest of the night. We were reasonably sure that it was her appendix, but she was never bothered with that pain again.

After being in the church now for a year, God began to bless us. It was 1954, and everything seemed to be going well for us. We were able to get a buyer for our house in Hickory, North Carolina and purchase a house in Baltimore, Maryland.

Next, we were also able to take our annual vacation out west to the home of my wife's sister, Frankie. She had married my Navy buddy, Lewis Correll, who now worked for the Northern Natural Gas Company. This company required them to move ever so often from place to place between Kansas and the panhandle of Texas. It became the highlight of every summer for us to spend my week's vacation traveling to visit them. I would load up my family and drive straight through from Baltimore, Maryland to their house, which was a distance between fourteen hundred and fifteen hundred miles.

Later in this same year of 1954, my daughter and I were having sore throats continually. We were both examined by a surgeon, and he informed us that we both must have our tonsils removed. We both entered the hospital and had a tonsillectomy at the same time. My dear wife stayed with us and held our daughter all night. The next morning the nurse came in and said to me, *"Hold on to my arm and see if you can stand by yourself."* I said, *"I have already been up and gone to the men's room."* She said, *"Get out of that bed and get dressed!"* My daughter even healed much quicker than I did.

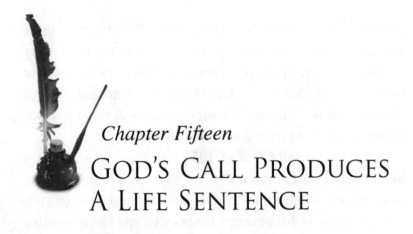

Chapter Fifteen

GOD'S CALL PRODUCES A LIFE SENTENCE

Sickness Strikes

From the moment I got saved, I applied myself to much study and prayer. After being in the church for two years, I began to feel deep in my spirit that God was preparing me for some type of work. However, I told the Lord that I would be a faithful saint, but I certainly would not be able to preach.

I was shy and timid about standing up in front of people. Even in school, I could not give a book report in front of my class. The teacher would let me come after school and give the report to her instead of giving it to the whole class.

In August of 1955, I began to get real sick. There were terrible pains in my stomach, and anything that I would eat, except raw eggs in milk with a little sugar and vanilla flavor, gave me severe pain. Finally, in December, I went to see Doctor Platt in Essex, Maryland, and he sent me for x-rays.

When I returned to his office for the results, he asked me if I had any children. I informed him that I had a seven-year-old son and a five-year-old daughter. He had a pencil in his hand that he threw down hard on the floor. When the eraser hit the floor, that pencil bounced across the room.

Then, he asked me why I had waited so long to come to him, and proceeded to inform me that his news for me was not good. He told me that I had a large tumor in my esophagus area that appeared very suspicious, and I would need to have surgery.

I asked the doctor how serious this was, and whether I would recover and regain my health. He informed me that it looked very serious, but he would not know the extent of it until he performed the surgery. He told me that I might not have more than a five percent chance of survival, and without the surgery I would probably not survive more than six months. His explanation was actually a death sentence, because he was giving me no more than six months to get done what I needed to do.

I thought that his prognosis and percentages were not very good. The doctor prescribed some strong medication to take for pain. Then, I was told to return for more x-rays in three weeks.

The church body began praying, and as I prayed, I questioned God concerning this illness. My children were small and my family needed me. I could not understand why this was happening to me since I had surrendered my life to the Lord and was now serving Him.

Another Vision

My wife was working the evening shift, and I was on the day shift. My father-in-law lived with us and took care of the children for two hours between the time my wife left for work and when I arrived home. He made himself available any time we needed him to.

One evening I did not feel well, and I told my wife's dad that I was going to lie down for a little while. As I lay across the bed, I began to pray. Then, I began to feel the presence of the Lord in that room. Speaking to the Lord, I told Him that whatever He wanted me to do, I would do it by His help.

I entered into a vision. In this vision, I was on an operating table and there were two doctors over to one side of the operating room conferring with each other. They both had on surgical masks and surgical clothes. On the wall was a blackboard, and this board began to glow with five words appearing as follows: **"This sickness is unto death."**

After the vision, I was perspiring, and I began to inquire of God. As I was laying there on that bed, knowing that my family needed me, I said to the Lord, *"I don't understand why this is happening to me since I am now serving You and striving to be obedient to Your will."*

I heard the voice of the Lord speak to my spirit. He said, *"I have called you to preach my Word. If you will heed this calling and put your trust in Me, I am all powerful and the Lord that will heal you; but, if you put your trust in medical science and not follow my will for your life, the end result will be death."*

I immediately got off the bed, took my very expensive medicine and threw it away in the toilet. I said, *"Lord, I commit myself into your hands. I am willing to do what You have called me to do. I am putting my complete trust in You. I know I cannot preach. If You want me to preach, You will have to preach through me."*

Prayer of Faith

The following Sunday evening we had a visiting minister to stop by our church by the name of Bishop M. K. Forbes from Kingsport, Tennessee. I had never met nor seen this man before. Our pastor, Reverend Frank Phelps, asked him to minister in this service. He greeted the congregation. Then, he stated that God spoke to him to have a prayer line, because there was someone there that needed a healing in their body.

Many in the congregation lined up to be prayed for including me. As the people began to come before him one at a time, the Spirit of the Lord began to move greatly upon the people.

There were approximately twenty people in front of me, but when my turn came, the minister asked me, *"Brother, what seems to be your problem?"* I replied, *"I have some stomach pain, which could be from ulcers."* He said, *"No, you do not have ulcers. While you were standing in line, the Lord permitted me to see inside of you. You have a serious malignant tumor in your esophagus area. The doctors are giving you six months or less to live. I'm not saying this to frighten you, but to let you know what God is going to heal you from tonight if you will believe Him to do so."*

I knew that no one had told Bishop Forbes this, because I had not even told my wife much less anyone else what the doctor had told me. The only ones that knew the doctor's prognosis was God, the doctor and me. This elevated my faith that the Lord had revealed this same prognosis to this man of God. So, when he prayed for me with my faith running high, I felt a warm burning sensation go through my whole body. I knew beyond the shadow of doubt that I was completely healed.

On the way home I told my wife and Aunt Lottie that God had healed me and they rejoiced. However, before we arrived home, another pain hit my stomach which almost doubled me over. I pulled over and stopped the car. I placed my hand on my stomach and said, *"Satan, you are too late! Jesus has healed me!"* That pain immediately began to leave my body. From that moment, I began to mend. I was now able to eat different foods, which I ate a little at a time. I proclaimed my healing to my family and the church, but I returned on schedule for more x-rays. I wanted my healing to be confirmed and documented by medical science.

After this second set of x-rays was completed, Doctor Platt told me that he would call me with the results. I waited by the phone for a call that never came. So, I called him to find out what was going on. He told me to come to his office to discuss my situation.

When I walked into his office, he had both sets of the x-ray pictures before him. His words to me were, *"My office is in a state of confusion. Specialists from Johns Hopkins Hospital have looked over both sets of x-rays of your stomach that were taken weeks apart and we don't understand. On the first set of x-ray pictures the tumor is quite visible, but on the last set of x-ray pictures everything is clear. There is no sign of any tumor.*

Addressing the doctor, I said, *"Brother, I was prayed for, and God has healed me."* Doctor Platt looked astonished and said, *"Well, something miraculous has surely taken place,"*

The devil tried to put that sickness back on me for a year or more. Periodically, without warning, a terrible pain would almost double me over. But, every time a pain would hit my stomach, I would put my hand on the pain and say, *"Devil, you are too late, because Jesus has already healed me."* Almost immediately that pain would start leaving my body. Eventually, all of that pain completely left me and never returned. I give all the glory to God.

During this time, I was having a real problem with my nerves that caused my shoulders to have a jerking reaction. Somewhere, during this period of my life, I realized one day that I was not jerking any more. Thank God, He had healed me of this problem, too, and no longer was I ever bothered with this anymore. All of the frightening dreams that I had been having were gone. The Scripture informs us *"... That every-thing God does will endure forever; nothing can be added to it and nothing taken from it..."* (Ecclesiastes 3:14 NIV)

My First Sermon

A short time later the pastor surprised me on a Sunday evening when he asked me to minister to the congregation on the following Saturday evening. I studied and prayed seriously that week, and I had what I thought was a good outline of notes. During service on Saturday night, I felt good and confident when the pastor invited me to the pulpit.

After opening my Bible and reading a Scripture, I looked over to my notes, and I could not see one note. I looked at the congregation, and every thought that I had disappeared. I stood there a couple of minutes and, then, said, *"Pray for me"* and sat down thinking that I would be the laughing stock. But, no one laughed, and the pastor covered for me really well, stating that they should have seen him the first time he stood up to minister.

I wanted to yell that I would never try to minister again, but I remembered the promise that I made to the Lord, *"I will do whatever You want me to do."* A short time later, the pastor asked me to speak again, and I consented to do so. Surprisingly to me, the Lord blessed, and I did quite well.

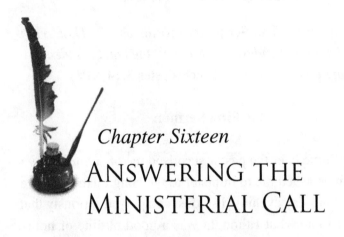

Chapter Sixteen

ANSWERING THE MINISTERIAL CALL

Local Ministerial License

After speaking several more times in our church, Pastor Frank Phelps slipped a paper in my hand one evening and asked me to read it prayerfully. When I arrived home, I opened the paper up and saw that it was an application for a local minister's license. I told the pastor that I didn't feel like I was ready to take that step, and he said, *"I think you are, because I can see that God has His hand upon you."*

I was afraid to say no, so I proceeded to fill in the application. I was approved for a ministerial local license to preach the gospel. I continued to assist my pastor and was thoroughly enjoying the blessings of the Lord upon our local church body. Everything seemed to be going great.

One particular Sunday night the Lord was moving in our midst in an awesome way. People were in the Spirit dancing and running in the aisles. A widow lady by the name of Sister Medkins, who prayed much and was very close to the Lord, stood up in that service and said to the pastor, *"Brother Frank, tonight I had a vision, but I don't know what it means. I saw an angel appear, and its wing rested upon your shoulder. Then, it left you and moved over and settled its wing on Brother McIntyre's shoulder."*

I was troubled by her vision, so the next day my wife, children and I went to see Sister Medkins. When we arrived at her apartment, we learned that she had left that morning to go to Ohio to live with her children. We never saw her again.

We continued to have great services for several months until a major problem arose in the church. Pastor Phelps resigned and walked out of the church. A great number of the saints who were family–connected to the pastor left with him. This was heart breaking to me, because I thought very highly of the pastor.

Pastoral Duty

There was a small number of people that remained in the congregation, and we gathered often and prayed that the Lord would send us another pastor. Some of the people contacted the bishop of our small organization seeking his advice in obtaining a new pastor. To their surprise, he suggested that they choose me as their pastor.

When they told me his suggestion, I was left almost speechless. I certainly did not feel qualified to lead a flock of people as their pastor. But, in February of 1957, I was officially installed as the pastor of this church. It was then that I realized the fulfillment of Sister Medkins vision.

This was the same church that my wife and I had become converted and given our hearts to the Lord in. I was ordained in March of 1957. I felt like a child whose mother had passed away, and I was left to care for a group of younger siblings. I made numerous mistakes, but the Lord and the people were patient with me. It didn't take long for us to experience the blessings of the Lord with new people being added to the church.

Our church met in a nice hall on the second floor of an old former men's clothing storefront building called Gann's, which was located in South Baltimore, Maryland. There was no air conditioning, so we raised the windows to get fresh air. When the piano, guitars and tambourines began to play, and the saints raised their voices to sing, we could be heard for quite a distance. It drew people in close to either worship with us or to oppose us.

Angry Neighbors

Many people in the neighborhood of the church were Catholic, and they did not appreciate us Pentecostals being in the community. Some of them would gather in the alley alongside our church and try to make enough noise to shut us down, but that did not work. In fact, it seemed as though our people just worshipped much better when this happened. At times, some of our opposition would slip up the stairwell and throw ripe tomatoes or raw eggs at us. At other times, they would throw them through the open windows, and they did not always miss their target.

My son, Terry, always sat in front of a large window near the platform, and his best friend, Edward ("Eddie") Tomlinson, sat beside him. However, for some reason on this particular Sunday night, they had switched places. The music and singing were highly anointed in making a joyful noise. People had filled the front of the church and were shouting and worshiping the Lord.

Eddie happened to look down and saw that his shoe was untied. Just as he bent over to tie his shoestring, half of a cement block came through that window right over his head. As it hit the floor, it bounced and rolled all through the shouting people, but it never hit anyone. Glass went all down Eddie's shirt collar, but he never got one cut. Without a doubt, if he had not bent over to tie his shoe, that cement block would have hit him in the back of the head and would have killed him. Thank God for His protection.

Our building was old and dry as a powder keg. One night, some of the people piled newspaper on the stairwell and set it on fire. When we were descending the stairs after service, we discovered the charred paper, but the fire had gone out without causing any damage. If this building had caught on fire, some handicapped elders probably would not have been able to exit the building. This was proof of how much these people actually disliked us being there.

One Sunday night we were leaving church after having a tremendous service. As we walked outside, an angry lady met me at the exit door and said, *"We cannot watch our television programs, because of the noise you people are making. You are going to have to stop that noise."* I said, *"We do not consider it noise. We call it worship, and I am sorry if it offends or disturbs you."* She said, *"You call that worship?"* I said, *"Yes ma'am, that is exactly what we call it."*

As I walked on across the street to our car, her son (in his thirties) came running at me with his fist drawn back, and my son said, *"Dad, I think this man wants to see you."* I turned around just as the man caught up with me, smiled at him and said, *"May I help you?"* The man stopped dead in his tracks, dropped his fist, began to tremble and muttered, *"I'm sorry"* and walked away.

On another Sunday night Eddie Tomlinson's mother, Lillian Tomlinson, came to me and said, *"Brother McIntyre, Eddie has a growth on his thumb. When I took him to be checked out, the doctor informed me that they were almost certain that it is malignant. It seems as though my faith is weak. Would you use your faith and pray for Eddie?"*

I anointed Eddie with oil and prayed for him. The next day as she was washing his hands before he went to school, she did not see the growth on his right thumb. Thinking she had the wrong hand, she checked the thumb on his left hand. There was no growth there either. When she realized the growth was gone, she started praising the Lord.

Secular Jobs Along with Being Pastor:

Glen L. Martin Aircraft Company

In January of 1958 with the ending of the Korean War, there came a large layoff at the Glen L. Martin Aircraft Company, which included me also. Jobs were rather scarce at this time, and I would park my car and walk around seeking employment. I checked out the places that advertised "Help Wanted," but I would receive the same message from all of them: *"Sorry, but if Martins calls you back, we are sure that you would leave us and go back to them."* I knew that this was just a testing time and, in due season, I would find a job.

Route Salesman for Rice's Bakery

A company named "Rice's Bakery" advertised for route salesmen needed to make home deliveries. This company delivered bread and other baked goods to individual houses. I made up my mind that I was going to be hired as I went to their employment office. I was interviewed by a Mr. King. He said that he would love to hire me, but it cost money to train a man for him to quit. He went on to say, *"When Martins calls you back, you will go, and I cannot blame you for returning to Martin's."* I said, *"Mr. King, I need this job, and if you hire me, I promise you that I will not leave you to return to my former place of employment."* Mr. King said, *"Alright, go and complete the paperwork and we will see you on Monday."* One month later Martin's did send me a recall letter, which I ignored.

My job at Rice's Bakery demanded a very heavy schedule on Saturdays. Since we also had church services on Saturday evenings, I told my field manager that I had to take my son in the truck to help me finish my route on Saturdays. I knew that the company was very strict about permitting anyone to ride on the truck besides employees of the company, because of insurance policies. However, the field manager never told me not to take my son on the truck, but asked me to keep it quiet and not to bring my son into the shop for the other drivers to see him. My son was well liked and ended up having his "own" customers that tipped him and gave him monetary gifts during the Christmas holidays.

Life Underwriter for
Sunlife Insurance Company of America

After working sixteen months for Rice's Bakery, God opened another door for me that I never saw coming. One of my customers by the name of Charles Taylor was a life underwriter for the Sunlife Insurance Company of America. I had always collected for their Rice's Bakery bill from Mr. Taylor's wife. But, on a certain day that I stopped by to collect for their bill, Charles was home. This was the first time I had ever met him.

I found Charles to be a real friendly man and after we talked a short while, he said to me, *"Mr. McIntyre, we really appreciate your service, and your job is a real respectful and needful job. But, I was wondering if you have ever considered becoming a life insurance debit underwriter?"* I said, *"It has crossed my mind, but I have not given it any serious thought."* He said, *"I think you would really like the work, and it would be a financial increase, also."*

He gave me a card with the insurance manager's name and phone number on it. When I came to a phone-booth, I stopped and gave this manager a call. The name of the manager was Mr. Respez. He answered my phone call and was very cordial on the phone with me when I introduced myself. He wrote down my information and thanked me very much for my call. He, then, said, *"I will be in touch with you in the near future."*

Three weeks later, Mr. Respez did contact me, and I was hired and trained as an agent for the Sunlife Insurance Company of America. This was my last secular job that I worked before the church grew financially to where I went full time at my second pastorate. This was the First United Pentecostal Church of Baltimore, Maryland located in Essex, Maryland that I founded in June of 1965.

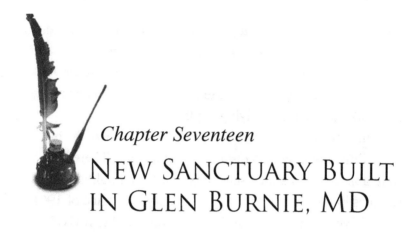

Chapter Seventeen

NEW SANCTUARY BUILT IN GLEN BURNIE, MD

While still pastoring in the city in South Baltimore, the church began to grow. We thought it was time for us to leave South Baltimore and relocate our church. We were able to purchase a nice plot of land in Glen Burnie, Maryland.

The former owner had felled the trees, and the lot was full of these trees and brush. I, along with two of the brethren from the church, went out to the lot on a Saturday to attack these trees and endeavor to saw them up with a chainsaw. The owner that we had purchased this lot from owned other property very near to our lot. He happened to have a large bulldozer clearing a lot close by.

One of the brethren had gone to purchase some more gasoline for the chainsaw. I said to the other brother, *"You be in prayer while I go up and talk to this bulldozer driver. I am going to ask him if he will come down and push all these trees into a large ditch on the backside of our lot."*

When I approached the man about doing this for us, he said, *"I have to get this lot cleared; therefore, I cannot do that."* I said, *"At lunch time if you would come down with this large bulldozer, you could push all these trees into that ditch and have the lot cleared in less than thirty minutes and, really, you will be doing this favor for the Lord. And, He would really bless you for doing it."* He started the bulldozer and continued his work there without saying anything.

But at twelve o'clock, I heard him coming down the hill. In just a little while, he had our lot nice and clean. Therefore, we were able to build a nice sanctuary and began holding revival services in the basement of this sanctuary in August of 1961.

On Wednesday, August 8th, 1961, during this revival, my son, Terry, at the age of thirteen was among the first to repent in our new building along with his best friend, Eddie Tomlinson. In fact, a young lady by the name of Sandy Shipley, Eddie's cousin, saw Terry crying and under much conviction. She began to tell him that what he was feeling was God and encouraged him to pray. The next thing he knew was that he was at the altar seeking God.

On Sunday, August 12th, 1961, we scheduled a baptismal service. The evangelist, Reverend Jack Forbes, was staying with us, and when we arrived home after service on Saturday evening, my daughter, Karen, at the age of ten, said, *"I want to be baptized, too."* The evangelist said, *"Honey, you can repent right here."* Big tears started running down her cheeks. She fell on her knees and started praying. I looked at my mother and said, *"Mom, if you would like, I will baptize you, also."* Mom said, *"Son, I am thinking about it."*

When Sunday, August 12th, 1961, rolled around, mom came out of her room carrying her baptismal clothes. I was privileged and thrilled to baptize my son, Terry, daughter, Karen, and my mother, Dessie Watson, along with nine other people in the name of the Lord Jesus Christ in the Chesapeake Bay.

The Lord was also blessing us in our new location with new people beginning to attend our services. It was thrilling to see people respond to the Word of God, kneel at the altar to pray and be blessed as the Holy Ghost would move upon them. The following are some notable things that happened after moving into our new sanctuary:

One middle-aged couple by the last name of Cubbage started attending services, and both of them would come forward and pray very sincerely. I discerned that the lady had a real problem of demon possession. When she would pray, suddenly, her voice would change. I asked the saints to fast and pray before the next service for this couple.

In the next service, I asked Sister Cubbage to come forward, so we could pray for her. As we prayed, I began taking authority over every unclean spirit, when all of a sudden, her voice changed and said, *"I know who you are Ralph McIntyre. You are a good man. There are seven of us here, and you don't have the power to cast us out."* I said, *"No, but I know the One who can. In the name of Jesus Christ, I take authority over every unclean spirit tormenting this woman. I command you to depart now."*

Sister Cubbage was a small frail woman, but she became powerfully strong when these demonic spirits rose up in her. When this would happen, four big strong men could hardly prevent her from overpowering them. However, when I commanded them in the name of Jesus to depart from her body, immediately, she went limp and fell to the floor. The demons had to leave through the power of the name of Jesus. I took her by the hand and lifted her up, and she began to speak in tongues as God baptized her with His Holy Spirit. We rejoiced over this miraculous deliverance.

We had a lady in the church by the name of Helen Smith who had a friend that was home–bound and wanted to have a Bible study. The next week my wife and I met Sister Smith and proceeded to the lady's apartment. The lady was thrilled that we had come. At the close of our very interesting Bible study, we began praying for this lady. She tearfully repented. Then, she asked, *"Reverend, is there any way that I could be baptized?"* I realized that she was very serious in making a commitment to follow Jesus. She was a small lady, and I said unto her, *"If you desire to be baptized this evening, Sister Smith can assist you, and we will baptize you in your bathtub now."* She readily agreed.

When I baptized her by immersion in the name of the Lord Jesus Christ for the remission of her sins, she sat up out of the water, raised her hands and began to thank and praise the Lord in beautiful worship. Suddenly, she began to speak in another language as the Lord baptized her with the Holy Spirit. I am very thankful that we baptized her that evening, because she passed away the next week and went to her reward.

United Pentecostal Church Affiliation

The small organization that I was a part of consisted of only six churches that were many miles apart in distance. It was a good fellowship, but there was not enough strength to reach out and accomplish anything much more than our own personal needs.

Late in 1962 I became acquainted with a minister by the name of Tommy Williams. He was a pastor in Wilmington, Delaware affiliated with the United Pentecostal Church (UPC). He invited me to preach a sectional rally at his church. At this rally, I met around twenty ministers of the UPC. I was highly impressed and began to gather information on this organization.

I found out that their manual of beliefs was consistent with what I believed.

I contacted Reverend Williams again after studying the Manual of the UPC to set up a meeting with him. At this meeting I inquired as to what procedure there was to become affiliated with the UPC. He presented an application to me and said, *"You have to fill out one of these and send it to the district board that oversees your territory. Then, they will notify you when their next board meeting is and have you meet with them."*

Glancing through the application, I said, *"According to this, an ordained minister of the organization has to sign the application recommending the candidate. No one in the UPC knows me."* He said, *"I know that you are a man of God, and I will be glad to sign the application for you."*

After completing the application, I mailed it to the address that he provided. Shortly after sending in the application, the secretary of the East Central District of the UPC received my application. He mailed me a letter of invitation to meet the board in Parkersburg, West Virginia in March of 1963.

A brother from my congregation by the name of Newlan Coleman traveled with me to meet the board, and we were given a very warm welcome. After explaining my burden and work as a minister, the members of the board questioned me extensively. Then, they asked me to excuse myself for a short period of time. After their discussion of me, the board called me back in and gave me a hearty welcome into the organization. They informed me that they had approved me as a minister in the United Pentecostal Church (UPC) and agreed to accept my ordination as a transfer from the organization that had previously ordained me.

I attended my first East Central District Conference in May of that year (1963) at what was known as the West-End Church in Huntington, West Virginia. Reverend David A. Robinson was the host pastor. The sanctuary had just been completed, and it was beautiful. After those meetings, I knew that I had made the right decision in becoming part of this great fellowship.

Prior to our affiliation with the UPC, we had no other churches to have fellowship with, because the other churches in our former organization were too far apart. After becoming part of the UPC, Reverend Orville Overton started a Home Mission church in Bel Air, Maryland, and Reverend Carl Gardner started a work in Washington, D.C., which gave us some fellowship in close proximity to our church in Baltimore, Maryland (Glen Burnie area). This was the beginning of a numerical growth of UPC churches in the Maryland and Washington, D.C. area of our country.

A Notable Miracle in The Glen Burnie Church

We had an elderly sister in the church by the name of Ella Koontz, who had come with us when we left the Glen Burnie church. Everyone called her Aunt Ell. She had several health ailments. On one occasion while I was still the pastor of the Glen Burnie Church, my mother was visiting with us when Aunt Ell called stating that she was very sick. I told her that we would come immediately to pray for her.

We lived eleven miles from her, and when we arrived at her house, she couldn't even get up. The door was unlocked, so we walked in. She was lying lifeless on the bed. My mother was a practical nurse. She looked at Aunt Ell who was turning blue. She checked her vitals and said, *"Son, she is gone."* I took Aunt Ell by the hand and said, *"Aunt Ell, we are going to pray for you."* We began to pray, and I felt the presence of the Lord. Suddenly, life and coloring came back into her body, and she got on her feet and began to dance and worship God. We all rejoiced in the Lord over this miracle. In fact, I believe this miracle is what made a believer out of my mother and was influential in her getting baptized in Jesus' name.

The church in Glen Burnie, Maryland where I was pastoring had grown, and we now had in attendance between eighty and one hundred people on any given Sunday. However, heavy friction began to appear in our midst. This church had its beginning with three or four ladies gathering together to have prayer meetings. Two or three other ladies had joined them, and at that time, they had sought a pastor for their small group. Brother Frank Phelps had accepted the invitation to join them as their pastor, and people were added to the small congregation as God began to bless.

But, the devil created some problems causing Pastor Phelps to resign as their pastor. With my election as the next pastor, it didn't take long for the honeymoon to be over. As time moved on, it was becoming more difficult for me to pastor a number of these folks, because many of them belonged to the same pioneering family and (in my opinion) wanted everything to go their way. I was in a quandary as to what to do, because I did not want to move outside of the will of the Lord.

My wife and I loved these people very much. However, I was feeling led to resign as the pastor, but my wife did not want to leave them. These were people that had helped pray us through to the Holy Ghost when we first started going to church. I began to fast and pray for divine direction.

One night I had a dream. This dream revealed to me that there was something wrong with our church building. In this dream, I had called in a builder to inspect it. The builder began to look things over. I never one time saw the builder's face.

In this dream, the builder stated that the problem was in the foundation. I inquired as to what we could do to remedy the problem. He said that when the problem is in the foundation, it is very difficult to correct the situation. Then, without another word, the builder disappeared without supplying me with a solution. I always believed that the builder in that dream was the Lord or an angel that He had dispatched.

Resigning as Pastor of The Glen Burnie Church

I was feeling that the Lord wanted me to resign as pastor of that congregation, and I felt that He was leading me to go across town and build another home mission church for Him. I continued to pray, *"Lord, if it is your will for me to make this move, then, speak to my wife's heart about leaving, also."*

One day right out of the blue, my wife said, *"You know, maybe it is the Lord's will for us to leave this church."* I began to praise the Lord and said to my wife, *"I know that it is the will of the Lord for us to resign, and I have been praying that He would reveal this to you."*

I called a special meeting to take place on Sunday, May 16th, 1965 at 6:00 PM, and twenty–four voting members attended. I explained to the people that the church had two opposing sides that were divided right down the middle, and that I had called this meeting for a pastoral vote of confidence. We cast secret ballots for this vote. When the vote was counted, it resulted in a tie. Twelve people (most from the same family) voted for me to resign, and twelve people voted against me resigning as the pastor. It could not have been equally divided any more than that.

As I Addressed the congregation, I said, *"One-half of you wants to go one way, and the other half wants to go another way. The church will never prosper in that state. Therefore, I am submitting my resignation tonight to take effect on May 30th, 1965. Now, to you that desire my resignation, we have approximately twenty-five hundred dollars in cash in the bank. All of us have contributed to the church building and the cash on hand. We should not depart as enemies, but as brothers and sisters in Christ. I will give you the cash and extra chairs for you to go where you would like to go and start your own work, and I will keep the new building. On the other hand, if you would prefer the building, then, I will take the money and chairs and relocate to start another church across town."*

I suppose I used a little reverse psychology, because I did not want the building. I knew the Lord was leading me to another area approximately twenty miles in distance from them, but I knew that they desired the building.

They readily agreed to take the new church building and give us the money and old folding chairs. I made two hard copies of this agreement with every voter's name on both, and I had every voter to sign both copies. I gave them a copy and I kept a copy to diffuse any misunderstanding.

During this time, I was working as a life insurance underwriter, and the next day after our church meeting, I went on my debit. One of my clients by the name of Mrs. Murphy wanted to know if she could ask me a question. I said, *"Sure, Mrs. Murphy."* She said, *"I was told that you stole all the church money and ran off with it."*

I started laughing. Then, I pulled out the copy of the agreement and read it to her along with all the signed signatures. She said, *"Thank you, Brother McIntyre! I know you too well and knew that there had to be an explanation to what took place. In my heart, I knew that you had not done what I had heard."*

Most everyone on my insurance debit knew that I was also a minister, so I thanked God for prompting me to draw up this agreement to protect the character and integrity of the ministry and my name.

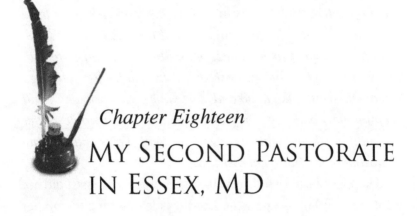

Chapter Eighteen

MY SECOND PASTORATE IN ESSEX, MD

After leaving the Glen Burnie church, we worshipped with Brother Overton in Bel Air, Maryland for a couple of Sundays, but I knew that if I did not find a place of our own very soon, the few people, (approximately twenty), that made up our new congregation would become restless.

After searching for several days during the latter part of June, I spotted a "For Sale" sign on an old dilapidated house in Essex, Maryland. This house sat on a nice piece of property in a very good location.

We checked with the zoning board and discovered that we would be permitted to build a sanctuary on this property. So, we purchased the property at a very reasonable price. We did some renovations on the house and were able to hold our first service there on August 1st, 1965.

The lot was rather large and had weeds about three feet high. I called a meeting with the brethren on a Saturday and informed them that we had to get rid of those weeds. They replied that this would be a tough job. I informed them that I didn't think it was going to be too hard. I placed them all around the lot and set it on fire. The blaze of the fire went very high in the sky, but everything went well.

The Lord blessed our efforts, and visitors began showing up for service. Some folks came out of curiosity, but there were other folks that were hungry for God and began to repent and receive the Holy Ghost baptism.

Then, we found ourselves facing another problem. We needed a baptismal pool to baptize the new converts. I happened to mention this need to a fellow life insurance underwriter by the name of Harry Rainer. Harry said, *"I can solve that problem. I am one of the head honchos at our community beach in our neighborhood and give you permission to baptize there."*

All I had to do was call him anytime there was a convert to be baptized, and he certainly saw to it that we had a group of people to witness the baptism, because he always announced to the neighborhood that the Pentecostals were coming for baptisms. They couldn't believe that anyone would be crazy enough to go into that cold water in the dead of winter!

Our Children, Grandchildren and Great Grandchildren All Born Again

Through it all, we were able to put both of our children in music classes to learn to play instruments. Music has been a tremendous blessing to the ministry of our son, Terry. He blessed us as he spent many hours in our home playing the accordion, guitar and piano. Terry loved church services, and when I would preach out in other churches, he would accompany me. He also attended district conferences with me. Eventually, he and his wife became pastor and foreign missionaries to the countries of Kenya and the Fiji Islands.

Likewise, our daughter, Karen, dedicated her life to the Lord at a young age and married a preacher. They traveled for several years as evangelists all over the country conducting many revivals. Then, they became pastor of a church in Athens, Georgia. I am thrilled that both of my children are active in God's Kingdom to this present time.

I can never express in words how thankful I am that our two children, our four grandchildren and our seven great–grandchildren have all experienced the spiritual birth of water and the Spirit according to Acts 2:38. I am perpetually blessed.

My Mother and Her Children
(Ralph, Ellen, Mom, Lorene, Roy)
Easter 1965

First District Camp Meeting

In July of 1965 we attended our first district camp meeting at Point Pleasant, West Virginia. This was a new camp that did not, as yet, have any paved roads leading into it. It had rained hard, and we got part of the way into the camp and got stuck in the mud along with a number of other people. This was a setback, but it turned out to be a great camp meeting and our young people came home excited and on fire for God.

Elected Presbyter

I wanted to become more involved with the East Central District, so I made up my mind that I was going to start attending our annual district conferences. In May of 1966, I attended the conference in Weirton, West Virginia. This is a time when business is taken care of, such as, departmental promotions, election of officers, resolutions and so on. There are sectional presbyters that make up the district board along with the super-intendent and secretary/treasury.

To my amazement, I was elected by my fellow minis-ters to be the presbyter of our section, which included part of Maryland, part of Virginia and Washington, D.C. Most of the board meetings were held in West Virginia, which was a long and hard trip for me, but I enjoyed the work and the fellowship of the brethren.

One particular Monday I had to leave home quite early in the morning in order to attend a called board meeting in Harrisville, West Virginia. We worked diligently, but we had to work until 1:00 AM on Tuesday morning to complete our work. The pastor of the Harrisville, West Virginia church, Reverend Kenneth Perine, invited me to spend the rest of the night in their home. I thanked him for his kindness, but I informed him that I really had to return home, because of my secular job as a life underwriter. I had to be on the job that morning.

After traveling approximately three hours, I was very tired. As I approached Frederick, Maryland, I fell asleep. I don't know how long I was asleep, but, suddenly, it felt like someone shook me, and I became wide awake. I immediately saw this tractor and trailer about one hundred feet in front of me moving slowly up a mountain incline. In moments I would have run under the back of this trailer. I praised the Lord that I had awakened in time to possibly have avoided a tragic accident.

When I arrived home, my wife met me at the door. Her first words were, *"Are you alright?"* I said *"Yes! Why?"* She said, *"I had a bad dream that you were in great danger, and I prayed for you."* I said, *"What time did you have that dream?"* She said, *"It was five o'clock this morning."* That was exactly the time I felt that shake that woke me up. I definitely believe that was an angel that shook me in answer to my dear wife's prayers.

Not long after returning from West Virginia, my father-in-law, Blaine Houston, moved back to North Carolina and started a new business that consisted of a little gasoline station and country convenience store.

One Sunday a friend called and informed us that Blaine was in the hospital in a very critical condition. I called a minister friend, Pastor James Cornett, in Newland, North Carolina and requested that he would go to the hospital in Banner Elk, North Carolina and pray with Blaine. Although it was Sunday, a busy time for a pastor, he agreed to go.

My wife and I got on our knees and called upon the Lord. After a period of time, I spoke to my wife and said, *"Everything is going to be alright. God is going to raise Blaine up."* Then, we received another call that stated that Blaine was improving. That very week my wife, daughter and I made a trip to the hospital in North Carolina, and we were thrilled to find my father-in-law much improved from his surgery.

A year or so later my father-in-law was in conversation with my son and said, *"Let me tell you about my experience at the hospital. When the surgeon was operating on me, I felt my spirit leaving my body. I was up above the medical group looking down upon my body."* Then, he said, *"As I was ascending higher, I met someone clothed in solid white, but never saw His face who said, 'You will have to go back, because you have some unfinished business on earth to take care of."'*

My son thought for a little while, then said, *"Pawpaw, I can tell you what your unfinished business is. You need to repent, get baptized in Jesus' name and receive the gift of the Holy Spirit."*

In 1972, Blaine sold his business and came to live with us in Baltimore, Maryland. He started attending church services with us and after a short period of time, he came forward and began to pray. Several members gathered around to pray with him, and God baptized him with the Holy Spirit. My son, Terry, then baptized him in water in the name of the Lord Jesus Christ. What a thrill that was for all of us!

In 1974, we entered into a building program for our church by adding a second floor. At this time, my father-in-law became extremely ill with severe pain in his stomach area. His doctor in North Carolina was sending him medicine. One day he told my wife that he would like to return to Crossnore, North Carolina and enter the hospital there. I went into his bedroom and informed him that I would take him there on Monday. He stated to my wife that he hoped we were not too late.

We left at 10:00 PM that Monday evening and drove the five hundred miles arriving Tuesday morning. X-rays were made, and Doctor Smith set him up for some more pictures to be taken; but, Blaine told me that he was too weak to have them done, so I had them to cancel that procedure.

On Thursday, Doctor Smith called me outside and stated that his condition was terminal, so he had ordered a private room for him. On Friday evening, Blaine was looking around and reaching out. I told my wife, *"He is looking for you."* She said, *"Here I am, Daddy"* and took hold of his hand. Then, he reached out his other hand, and I took it. He kind of smiled at us and, then, went into a coma.

My wife and I were staying around the clock at the hospital, and some friends came on Friday morning and persuaded us to go with them to have some breakfast. Reluctantly, we went to the restaurant with them, which we enjoyed and appreciated. We returned to the hospital and decided to leave around 1:00 PM and refresh ourselves. As we were preparing to return to the hospital at 3:00 PM, I received a call from the nurse stating that my father-in-law had just passed away.

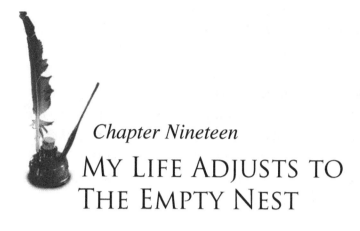

Chapter Nineteen

MY LIFE ADJUSTS TO THE EMPTY NEST

Off to Bible College

My son, Terry, graduated from high school in 1966. In his senior year, he was wrestling in his mind between attending Texas Bible College or attending the University of Maryland. Being very good at math, he was interested in pursuing a career in electrical engineering. But, God was dealing with him about Bible college.

One morning near the end of his senior year, he walked into his homeroom class. No one was there except for the teacher, Mr. Arthur Morton, who was also his academic math teacher. Mr. Arthur Morton, an African American, was Terry's favorite teacher of all the teachers he ever had.

Mr. Morton asked Terry what his plans were when he graduated. Terry assumed he would not understand if he told him he was thinking about a Bible college, so he said, *"I've given some thought to going into electrical engineering at the University of Maryland."* Mr. Morton replied, *"Boy, you don't want to do that. I had a nephew that went there and it ruined him. Why don't you think about a Bible college? I have observed you for two years. You come out of a very religious family, don't you? Are you Catholic?*

Mr. Morton had attended Loyola University of Maryland, a Catholic school, and was going to recommend it to him. Terry answered, *"No, I am not Catholic; however, my father is a Pentecostal pastor."* He said, *"I was sure you came out of a right religious family. I think you should seriously consider going to a Bible college."*

Terry came home and told my wife and me what had transpired. He said, *"I was in a quandary as to what I should do, but I believe God used Mr. Morton today to confirm to me that I should go to Bible college."*

So, that fall of 1966, he along with three other fine young men from our congregation, (Ed Lemke, Sam Lipscomb, David Rowswell), flew to Houston, Texas to attend Texas Bible College. I had felt all along that God had a call on his life, and that he should attend Bible college; however, I didn't want to influence him into doing my will for his life. I prayed for him and was well pleased concerning his change of direction, but we certainly felt the loss of the presence of all four of these young men in our services.

Young People Destroyed by Drug Culture of The Sixties

In the early sixties drugs had begun to be a real problem for a lot of young people. There were students in our schools that became runners for drug dealers. Many young people were being approached and getting involved. This was truly a work of Satan, causing many promising students to become addicts. Some of these students have overdosed and died a premature death. The minds of other students have been heavily affected.

Many parents back then and even today cannot understand why their children have taken the wrong road of life. They are blinded by Satan in not realizing that they have forgotten God and raised their children in the ways of a corrupt world. If you want to do right and have your children to do right, you must have Jesus in your life. Jesus is the difference and makes all the difference in the world.

My wife and I took time for our children, loved them, prayed with them and kept them faithful in attendance to the house of God. We are so very thankful to the Lord that our children never got involved in this way of life, but chose the life of true Christianity.

Building New Sanctuary in Essex, Maryland

I was able to obtain a set of blueprints for a small church building and took them to an architect. He placed his seal on them, and I submitted them to the zoning board to apply for a building permit. Our blueprints were passed by this board, and we were issued a permit to build a church. However, a problem arose when I found out that the company that we were planning to use to erect our building had gone out of business.

I met with the brethren and informed them about this problem. Due to the fact that we could not afford the asking price of other companies to build, I relayed to them that we were going to have to build the structure ourselves. Brother Carlton Brown asked, *"Are you a builder?"* I said, *"No, but I can read blueprints."* Sometimes, you just have to do what you can do to arrive at the final product.

So, in March of 1967, we began digging by hand our footer for the foundation. When we had about half of the footer trenches dug, a very heavy rain came and filled them with water.

Then, the temperature dropped into the twenties. Our trenches were full of water capped with ice.

We had three young men from the same family that had worked hard digging those trenches. When I arrived at the building site, they were in those trenches of water and ice, bare-footed and shoveling away. I demanded for them to get out of there immediately, which they did, reluctantly. I called a friend, and he borrowed three pairs of rubber boots, which made those young fellows very happy.

We used a submersible pump to get the water out and set our stakes. After inspection by the building inspector, we poured the footer. The ground was so soft that the concrete had to be transported about fifty feet from the truck by wheelbarrow.

I had observed block–laying, but I had never personally laid any blocks. In conversation with my neighboring pastor, Brother Orville Overton, I relayed to him that I was going to have to lay my own blocks. He readily volunteered to help me, and I asked him if he had ever laid any blocks. He replied, *"No."*

When I worked at the aircraft plant, I had worked with transits and levels. I borrowed a transit level from a builder. We squared and set all of the corners to the appropriate height. Then, we used a line level, and the project turned out rather well. I contracted the pouring of the concrete slab to a gentleman, and he stated that the foundation was not off more than one-quarter of an inch anywhere.

This project along with my other responsibilities took its toll on me physically. As a debit agent with the SunLife Insurance Company of America, I serviced my clients. As pastor of the church, I ministered in four services each week (Sunday morning, Sunday evening, Thursday evening and Saturday evening). As general contractor, I built the church sanctuary. I put in so many hours that at the completion of our sanctuary I became ill and had to remain in bed for several days.

We completed our building and moved into it in October of 1967. We obtained a permit to raze the old house. We decided, as we tore it down, that we would burn all the old lumber on our lot. We were placing small amounts of lumber at a time on the fire until an electrician, a friend of mine that was doing our electrical wiring, drug half of a side around and cast it on the fire. He said, *"Like the Indian, if you are going to have fire, have big fire."* The fire department was only about five hundred feet from our church, but we were glad that they did not show up.

Off to Bible College Again

Our daughter, Karen, decided to go to Texas Bible College in Houston, Texas, also. She went in the fall of 1968, which was two years after our son had gone. That spring of 1969 our son graduated from TBC. My wife and I drove from Baltimore, Maryland to Houston, Texas for the graduation week. We were able to spend the week visiting both of our children there.

While in Houston, Texas, Pastor James Kilgore, a renowned minister of a tremendous church (Life Tabernacle) in the United Pentecostal Church, invited me to preach to his congregation. It was a wonderful experience to be in the presence of this great man of God and an awesome privilege to minister in his great church.

1970 Marriage of Terry and Lynda

After graduation, Terry stayed in Houston for a couple of months and worked at Red Ball Motor Freight. Then, he drove from Houston, Texas to Tulsa, Oklahoma to see his dear friends, Gary and Delores Howard, before traveling to Huntington, West Virginia where I was scheduled to preach for Pastor Greene Kitchen. Beginning the next day was the East Central District youth camp and camp-meeting in Point Pleasant, West Virginia.

This is when and where Terry met his future life companion, Lynda Janelle White, in July of 1969. Her father, Lawrence (L.C.) White, was the pastor of a church in Spencer, West Virginia. After a period of time, they announced to us that they were planning to get married.

On June 11th, 1970 we traveled to Spencer, West Virginia for a wedding rehearsal that evening. The next day, June 12th, I officiated in their marriage ceremony and joined them together in Holy Matrimony.

A Notable Miracle in The Essex Church

After the wedding of my son and daughter-in-law was over, I asked the dear friends of my son, Gary and Delores Howard, from Tulsa, Oklahoma to come to Baltimore and preach for us that Sunday, June 14th, 1970. Gary had served as the best man in the wedding of my son and daughter-in-law.

A young man by the name of Harry Roark attended that Sunday evening service. He responded to the ministered Word of God by coming forth and kneeling at the altar. Some of the saints began to pray with him when, suddenly, evil spirits began to cause him to act boisterous and tossing him around. I asked a couple of the men to hold on to him to keep him from harming himself.

Then, I asked Brother Gary Howard to help me pray and cast these spirits out of this young man. Suddenly, he went limp and, then, began to rejoice and received the baptism of the Holy Spirit. He came to his feet, began to dance and speak out in other tongues as the Spirit gave him the utterance. He fell in love with the Lord and the church, and he was faithful for several years while he was with us before departing to Texas for college.

It was some time after his conversion that he was at the altar praying and worshipping. As he started to walk back to his seat, he lost his balance and stumbled over the altar. When he fell, he broke his arm. The bone was sticking up in his arm.

I was on my knees praying when my son said, *"Dad, Brother Harry just fell and broke his arm. He needs for you to pray for him."* I said, *"Saints this young man has broken his arm, let us join together in prayer."* As we began to pray, I was rubbing his arm very lightly when, suddenly, there was a snapping sound. Harry pulled his arm out of my hand and began to examine it. He raised it up without any pain and began to praise God. He exclaimed, *"Pastor, it is healed!"*

When he went home, he told his mother what had happened. She said to him, *"You are going to the hospital."* He said, *"I don't need to. The Lord has already healed me."* His mother said she was taking him to be checked anyway.

When his arm was x-rayed, the doctor came out and asked, *"Who set that arm?"* Harry explained what had happened to his arm, and the doctor said, *"The x-ray shows a complete break in the bone, but it has been set perfectly. You don't even need a cast. Just wear a sling for a couple of days, and you should be fine."*

Our Son's First Pastorate

In 1969 I was the Presbyter of our section in the East Central District of the United Pentecostal Church organization. There was a church in my section that needed a pastor. This church was located in Westminster, Maryland. With no pastor, I had to go minister there plus take care of the church that I pastored.

When my son returned to Baltimore after graduating from Texas Bible College, he offered to help me with this church in Westminster. He said, *"Dad, I do not feel any call from God to pastor that church, but if you would like, I will go there and help you out until you can find a pastor."* He stayed there from December of 1969 until April of 1972 as the pastor.

He went there before getting married and was there a couple of years after getting married. In 1972, he felt the burden lift from that place and decided it was time to resign and leave from there. However, he would not leave the people without a pastor. When he found a young minister, James Clonch, that was happy to go there and pastor, he left Westminster. I said, *"Son, if you are leaving there, I would like for you to come and assist me in the Essex church."* Thankfully, he agreed and was my Co-Pastor for fourteen and a half years.

1970 Marriage of Steve and Karen

In the fall of 1969, we went to our annual General conference that was held that year in St. Louis, Missouri. This is when and where our daughter, Karen, met a young man from Atlanta, Georgia by the name of Steve Cole.

It is rather humorous how I was introduced to Steve. While a number of us were gathered on a street corner fellowshipping, Steve joined the group. He was full of life and was bouncing around and stepped back on my toe. He immediately whirled around and began to apologize, and my daughter said,

"Steve, I want you to meet my Mom and Dad." Everyone began laughing at him.

But, as time progressed, they began to grow more serious in their relationship. We got hit with a double whammy that year as they announced to us that they were planning on getting married during their Christmas break from college.

On December 23rd, 1970 in Essex, Maryland, they were joined together in Holy Matrimony by Steve's dad, Reverend B.S. Cole, from Atlanta, Georgia.

After their marriage, they returned to Texas Bible College for Steve to complete his course of study for graduation. After evangelizing full time for a number of years, he became a pastor in Athens, Georgia where they reside today. They have built a beautiful church and pastor a church of some very fine people. Both of our children left the nest the same year, but we truly gained two more wonderful children in our family.

Mission Trip to Ecuador

In 1971 a great blessing came my way as it became possible for me to make a trip on the Foreign Mission field to Ecuador. Ecuador is a beautiful country in South America. Our Missionary, Reverend Daniel Scott, who was a very good friend of mine, invited me to Ecuador for their conference.

I preached the pre-conference service and some of the day services during the conference, and Reverend Paul Price from California preached the evening services. Brother Scott had never interpreted for anyone before, and I had never preached using an interpreter; but, we made a pretty good team.

After the conference we preached in several other churches in Ecuador. One special church that had just been completed was one that our church helped to build. We held the dedication service there on a Saturday night, and it was a thrill to preach there.

When the service started, it was raining lightly, and there were just a few people assembled. As the service progressed, people began to gather around. But, instead of coming into the building, they stood outside in the rain.

After I preached the message, it was exciting to see several of those people come in from the outside and make their way down to the altar. As the people were coming forward, Brother Scott leaned over and said, *"You have hooked a big fish."* He was referring to a certain man that received the baptism of the Holy Ghost. I later learned that he was the contractor and builder of that church building and other edifices.

I along with Brother and Sister Scott were traveling back to Quito, Ecuador late one night, and Brother Scott said, *"Brother Mac, I am very tired. Will you drive?"* He laid down in the back of the vehicle. Sister Scott was sitting up front, and we were talking as we moved along the road.

Suddenly, I heard a flapping sound and the ride became rough. I said, *"I believe we have a flat tire,"* and started to stop. Brother Scott raised up and said, *"Yes, we do have a flat tire."* The road where we were was pitch dark. Brother Scott said, *"I will get the jack."* In just a little time, I heard him say, *"We don't have a jack. Somebody has taken it."*

All we had was a nut wrench. It was so dark that you couldn't hardly see your hand in front of your face. I didn't know what to expect, so I took the wrench from Brother Scott and said, *"If you don't mind, I will hold on to the wrench."* It wasn't too long until we saw some head-lights. When it got close, we could see that it was a truck. Brother Scott waved for them to stop, but they kept going on by us.

However, they only went a short distance and stopped. Three fellows got out and came back to where we were. One of them said in Spanish words that meant, *"Having trouble?"* Brother Scott explained that we had a flat tire, and we discovered that someone had taken our jack. They happened to be real nice fellows and helped us.

In just a little time they had changed our tire. God is so very good. Brother Scott informed me later that where we had the flat tire was about a mile from where some head-hunters had killed several Catholic nuns some time ago.

Brother Scott was very sick for a couple of days during the conference. He could not eat anything and was becoming quite weak. Missionary Brother Battle was leading the service, and I leaned over and said to Brother Scott, *"I believe the Lord wants to heal you now. Go up and get prayed for."* He went to the platform, and when they prayed for him, he was immediately healed. We all praised the Lord for this touch and for all of the exciting experiences while I was there. I met some beautiful people in this great country.

Appointed as District Secretary/Treasurer

In May of 1967 at our district conference, Virginia was permitted to break off from the East Central District and become a Home Missions District. New churches began to form slowly in Maryland. By 1973 we had grown to ten churches and twenty-two ministers. In May of 1973 at our annual district conference, which was held in Baltimore, Maryland, I was appointed by the district board to fill the unexpired term of the district secretary/treasurer.

My wife and I traveled to Huntington, West Virginia and spent the night with Reverend Greene Kitchen, the newly elected superintendent who was the former secretary/treasurer. We went over the books and made arrangements for me to open a bank account in Essex, Maryland. The next day we loaded my car with a cabinet, receipts and office equipment. If I had known that Maryland would be permitted to form into its own district the very next year, there is no way I would have accepted the appointment as secretary/treasurer!

MARYLAND D.C. DISTRICT

Elected as the First District Superintendent of the Newly Formed District

First Maryland–D.C. District Board of the UPC
Alfred Asarisi, Presbyter – Herbert Reynolds, Secretary –
Ralph McIntyre, Superintendent – Roy Riffle, Presbyter –
James Shockey, Presbyter
(Left to Right)

The brethren of Maryland felt that we were able to become our own district. Gathering all of the required material, we sent it along with our petition to form Maryland and Washington, D.C. into its own district. This was all sent to our organization's headquarters in St. Louis, Missouri. Following the proper procedures, the General Board and West Virginia gave us approval.

On April 16th, 1974, Reverend S. W. Chambers, our General Secretary of the UPC, and Reverend Greene Kitchen, the District Superintendent of the East Central District, met in Essex, Maryland at the church I founded. The ministerial brethren of Maryland and Washington, D.C. came for this meeting. At the conclusion of this meeting, the Maryland/Washington, D.C. District was formed. It was at this time that the brethren elected me to be their pioneering superintendent of this newly formed district.

"Accelerated Christian Education" School Begins

In 1974, we entered into a building program for our church by adding a second floor, not realizing at the time how perfect this addition would be for a Christian school. The very next year of 1975 we became very interested in "Accelerated Christian Education." In the fall of 1976, we opened up our own ACE school that went from kindergarten through grade ten with eighteen students. The next year we added the eleventh grade, and our third year we added the twelfth grade.

We were fortunate to have Sister Hazel Lundy and Sister Maxine Warlick as Monitors, who started when the school was established and remained on the job throughout the school's ten-year existence. Our number of students grew until we were up to around fifty. We continued our school until 1986.

In the fall of 1985, my son informed me that they wanted to join the Foreign Mission Field of the United Pentecostal Church International. That was a shocker, but I had always taught my children to obey the Lord. I said that we would have to start planning to close the school, because it would be impossible for me to continue to operate it without Terry and Lynda carrying a lot of the load.

They received the news that they were approved under a five–year appointment as missionaries to Kenya, East Africa in May of 1986. Immediately after receiving this news, we sent out letters to the parents of all our students informing them that Essex Christian Academy would not be opening in the fall of 1986.

Degree: Doctor of Ministry

In 1978, I attended a meeting hosted by a representative from Drew University of Madison, New Jersey concerning pastors enrolling in a "Doctor of Ministry" program. It was a program of intense studies that required two to five years to earn the degree: "Doctor of Ministry."

This was a real challenge for me to undertake, but I enrolled, because I felt it was necessary due to me being principal of our Christian school. Many hours were required for study and research. Our studies commenced in the fall of 1978, and we had to spend two weeks on the campus of Drew University.

Then, the university sent professors to the Baltimore area, where we assembled in a Methodist Church in Millersville, Maryland for our class work. In January of 1980, we had to spend another week on the campus of Drew. The complete month of July had to be spent on campus, and due to our class work, we could not even return home on weekends. Many hours were spent in researching, studying and writing my dissertation. I was able to complete the course in thirty months and received the degree of "Doctor of Ministry" in Drew University's 113th graduation ceremony on May 23rd, 1981.

Ralph's Graduation at Drew University with Dr. Jones, My Advisor

During this period of time, my brother, Roy, was diagnosed with lung cancer. He came to see me and asked me for Scriptures that he could read. I gave him a list and told him not just to read them, but, also, to study them and pray.

He had surgery on his left lung. After he recouped, he did quite well for a while, but, disappointingly, cancer was discovered in his right lung. I did not encourage him to have surgery again, but while I was attending the UPCI General Board's midwinter meeting in Hazelwood, Missouri, he had his second surgery. This was followed by chemotherapy treatments. These treatments took their toll, and he grew very weak.

In November of 1981 we were having special services in our church. Roy attended these services, and God began to deal with his heart. When the invitation was given for all to come and pray, Roy was very weak, but he joined the group.

Several of the brethren were praying with him when, suddenly, in his weakened condition, he stood straight up with his hands raised and began to speak in other tongues. I said to him, *"Roy, I am going to baptize you!"* He said, *"Now?"* I said, *"Right now!"* And, he agreed. He kept growing weaker. He said, *"I would like for God to heal me, but if He decides not to, I know where I am going."* On February 27th, 1982 he went to be with the Lord.

Mission Trip to Thailand

Reverend Billy Cole, a former missionary to the country of Thailand, invited me to accompany him on his annual trip to minister in the Thailand Conference. The Maryland – D.C. District was wonderful to me by raising the funds to make it possible for me to accept this invitation.

In January of 1982, my son and my wife drove Brother Cole and me in an ice storm from Baltimore to the Reagan Washington National Airport near Washington, D.C. At that time this airport was known as the National Airport.

We flew out of this airport to San Francisco, California and spent several days in Stockton, California at the Christian Life Center where Reverend Kenneth Haney was the Pastor. Every year Pastor Haney hosted a conference called "Landmark," which was in session at this time. At his invitation, we ministered in this conference while we were there.

Then, we flew out of San Francisco on Japanese Air Lines (JAL) for Narita, Japan. We spent the night in Narita and flew on to Bangkok the next day. This trip was one of the highlights of my life. Brother Cole was a tremendous host and traveling partner.

In one of our Sunday morning services in Thailand, I witnessed thirty-two people receiving the baptism of the Holy Ghost in just a few minutes. Brother Cole was a man of great faith. I thoroughly enjoyed this trip and the wonderful experiences it afforded me.

Chapter Twenty

GOD'S FAITHFULNESS
IN DIFFICULT TIMES

Massive Heart Attack

On Monday December 23rd, 1985, my son and his family were leaving for West Virginia to visit with Lynda's parents for Christmas. I went by and picked up their small dog, Muggs, to take care of it for them. I drove the couple of blocks back to our home and told my wife that Muggs needed a bath. I ran water into the bath tub, sat down on the commode, washed the little dog and when I reached down to lift her out of the tub, a terrific pain hit me in the chest.

I dropped the little dog on the floor and said, *"I have a severe pain and need to go see the doctor."* My wife called our son and caught him just before they were leaving to visit Lynda's parents. He immediately came and drove me to my family doctor.

Doctor Louis Semenoff checked me. He told me to go straight to the hospital emergency room, and said, *"I will call them now to let them know you are on your way."* I tried to persuade my son and his family to continue on their trip, because I would be all right; but, they refused to leave me and cancelled their trip. I was admitted into Franklin Square Hospital and placed in the coronary care unit (CCU) around 1:00 PM. About three hours later (approximately 4:00 PM), I had a major thrombosis heart attack. If I had not been in the hospital, I probably would not have survived.

On Christmas day I was transferred from the Franklin Square Hospital to the Saint Joseph Hospital for catheterization and angioplasty. It was not possible to get a stent into the artery, but the blood rerouted itself, and this procedure was not necessary. The heart attack left me with only about one half of a functional heart from that day until this present time.

Terry, Lynda, Tawana & Blaine McIntyre

Missionaries to Kenya, East Africa

As mentioned earlier, Terry and his family were approved in May of 1986 by the Foreign Missions Board of the United Pentecostal Church International (UPCI) for a five–year appointment as missionaries to the country of Kenya, East Africa.

They began deputizing to raise their budget, traveling to many churches in many different states. They raised their budget in approximately seven months and were able to depart for their field of labor in June of 1987. They were sorely missed in our local church, and I personally missed Terry and Lynda's help. My wife and I both surely missed our grandchildren.

While attending our general conference on October 1st, 1987, the Foreign Missions Director, Reverend Harry Scism, invited my wife and me to be guests at their school of missions later that month. We were very happy to accept the invitation, which we enjoyed very much.

During our district camp meeting, our camp evangelist, Reverend Robert Mitchell, raised five thousand dollars to send my wife and me to Hawaii for a vacation. We appreciated his desire, but I expressed that we would rather go to Kenya to visit our children and grandchildren. He along with everyone else was glad to consent to our wishes.

In the latter part of January 1988, my wife, daughter and I made the trip and spent three wonderful weeks there. I was blessed to be the guest speaker in their annual General Conference and to teach in the Life Tabernacle Bible school in Kangemi (Nairobi area).

It was a great honor to minister to these precious people. We, also, thoroughly enjoyed going on the safaris and seeing the majestic animals of Africa and being able to view the beautiful countryside of this wonderful nation.

Resignation as District Superintendent

After returning home, I began having angina pains in my chest and spent several days in the hospital a couple of different times for a number of tests. During our district conference in April of 1988, I had an appointment with my cardiologist on that Wednesday. I informed him that our conference was presently convening, and I would probably be reelected to the office of district superintendent for another two years. He said, *"Reverend, you do not need that organizational pressure."*

I had been pondering whether I should let my name stand or to decline, and I felt that his statement was the confirmation and direction I needed to make my decision. So, when I returned to the conference, I had a meeting with the district secretary and a presbyter. I informed them that I was not letting my name stand for reelection. I had served the district for fourteen years as the founding superintendent.

Superintendent Honored

Frances, Ralph & Karen at Retirement
(Terry Called from Kenya, East Africa)

The brethren took it upon themselves to honor my wife and me on Thursday (the next evening) of the conference, which only gave them one day to prepare for the occasion. They arranged to fly my daughter to Baltimore, Maryland from Athens, Georgia. Attorney Owen Taylor and his wife met her at the airport and took her home with them until service time.

It was a real surprise when she came walking down the aisle with a dozen roses to present to her mother. Arrangements were made for our son, Missionary Terry McIntyre in Kenya, East Africa, to call from Kenya during the service and address the congregation. His call was connected to the church on the public address system in order that the congregation could hear the conversation. It was 3:00 AM in Kenya for him to call the church at 8:00 PM where we were in Maryland. It was quite a surprise to hear his voice in that service.

I was also directed to sit on the platform in a fancy new Lazy Boy recliner chair, and during the service, I was made aware that the chair was a gift to me from the district. Also, they gave us a nice love offering.

This was the superintendent's night of the conference to bring his annual message. My message for the evening was, *"How do you expect me to minister after all that you have done?"* They were happy for me to just respond to their kindness.

During the conference, the district bestowed upon me the honorary membership of the district board. At the General Conference held in Salt-Lake City, Utah in October of 1988, the General Board voted to make me an Honorary member of the General Board of the UPCI.

Ralph Resigning as District Superintendent of Maryland – D.C. in April of 1988

Quadruple Heart By-Pass Surgery

Late in April of 1988, I began having angina pains, and my cardiologist made arrangements for me to have a catheterization. Another cardiologist did the procedure and told my wife that he almost missed the arteries that were causing my problem.

When I returned to my cardiologist, Doctor Kenneth Lewis, for the results of the test, he said there didn't seem to be much change from my former exam. Then, my wife spoke up and said, *"Doctor Arnett, who performed the procedure, stated that he almost missed the arteries that were almost clogged."* Doctor Lewis looked astounded and then said, *"Reverend, this evening I will be going over your report and get back in touch with you."*

A couple of days later, Doctor Lewis called and informed me that he did not want me doing anything strenuous, because he had already made arrangements for me to have priority open heart surgery with June 13th, 1988 as a definite date, but, hopefully, sooner.

I called Doctor Lewis the next day and asked if I could give my own blood for the surgery. He said that would be fine as long as everything checked out physically okay. I said, *"Doctor Lewis, I don't mind waiting until June 13th for the surgery without the priority."* He said, *"Reverend, I would have you in there today if I could get you in, because you are prone to have another heart attack at any moment."*

On May 31st, I entered Saint Joseph Hospital in Towson, Maryland and underwent a quadruple by-pass heart surgery on June 1st, 1988. I gave a pint of blood every three or four days and was able to give four pints of my blood with the surgery only requiring three pints. The performing surgeons were Doctor MacDonald and Doctor Brawley. I spent twelve days in the hospital, because there was trouble in getting my heart to regulate properly.

It was truly good to be able to return home, but sitting around doing nothing during recovery was the hard part.

Doctor's orders were emphatic for me not to pick up anything that weighed over five pounds. The summer passed rather fast.

In October we were able to purchase the house and lot that joined our church property, and we started a renovation of our sanctuary with a new addition. I was back in the groove, working off a scaffolding, doing some spackling and doing some painting.

Wife Undergoes Surgery

In December of 1988, my wife had a physical problem and had to undergo surgery from which she had a slow and painful recovery. Through it all, she insisted on doing her work in the home and was faithful in attending the church services.

My wife was loved by everyone, because she always saw the good in everyone. She always had a nice word to say concerning all. She was a very wise person to say the least. I have been truly blessed to have had her as my partner and helper in the Lord.

In February of 1989, I returned home after working all day at the church cutting through a sheetrock wall and installing a door. While my wife fixed dinner, I carried the garbage out to the street for pickup. When I stepped onto our driveway, I thought I was stepping on snow, but it was solid ice instead. I began to slide and my feet went out from under me. When I landed on the ground, my left arm hit so hard that it broke.

When I came into the house, I informed my wife that I had taken a fall on the ice. She asked, *"Did you get hurt?"* I said, *"Yes, I broke my arm, but continue to fix our dinner while I shower and get rid of this sheetrock dust. The emergency room will probably be very busy and crowded. Anyway, I'm hungry."*

After taking care of my broken arm at Franklin Square Hospital, things eventually smoothed out, and we were moving along pretty much as normal until January of 1990. My wife, Frances, had a mammogram that appeared suspicious. A biopsy was prescribed, which proved to be malignant.

After the diagnosis of cancer, the surgeon made an appointment for my wife to have a radical mastectomy. She cancelled the appointment one day before the scheduled surgery. I said to her, *"I want the very best for you, but this is one decision that you will have to make all by yourself, because it is your body. However, I will back whatever you decide."*

I fasted and prayed for eleven days on her behalf. Many prayers were going up to the throne for her from many different people. Our son, Terry, was in special services in Ethiopia, and all of those people were praying for her.

Yet, there were some well-meaning and concerned people that tried to persuade my wife to follow through with the surgery. The surgeon and a gynecologist both called and tried to persuade her to change her mind. They told her that without surgery she would probably not survive more than three months at the most.

She decided to put her full trust in God. It paid off very well, because without the surgery, that pain left my wife and never returned. She lived over nineteen years longer, and her death was from a different ailment and not cancer. She was cancer-free.

Chapter Twenty-One

SHIFTING GEARS IN A NEW DIRECTION

Terry Receiving Pastoral Staff from His Mom and Dad

Passing the Pastoral Staff

I had been feeling that I needed to resign as pastor, because I seemingly did not have the strength anymore to perform the duties required. In fact, without talking to my son, I decided to have a meeting with our church congregation. I said to them, *"I don't know if my son and his wife would decide to resign as a missionary to Kenya, East Africa when their five–year*

215

appointment ends in 1991 or if they will decide to extend their appointment. However, if they would believe it to be God's will to terminate at the end of their appointment and return to this church, I would like to know how many of you would want them to become your pastor. I am going to take a secret ballot. Just write 'Yes' if you would be in favor of them becoming your next pastor or 'No' if you are opposed to them becoming your next pastor." When the ballots were collected, the result was unanimous with one hundred percent present voting "yes" in favor of them becoming the next pastor of the First United Pentecostal Church in Essex, Maryland.

I called Missionary Terry and told him what had transpired. He was surprised and humbled by the confidence of the members of the church. However, he told me that one year ago the Foreign Missions Division had appointed him as the Superintendent of Kenya, Rwanda, Burundi and Uganda, and they were very happy with the work that was taking place throughout East Africa. They planned on spending their lives there; but, he said that he and his wife would fast and pray about it. I told him that I would not want him to return unless he definitely knew it was God's will.

In the latter part of 1990, my son called me after he and his wife had spent considerable time seeking God's will about this situation. He said, *"As we sought God, He began to reveal to us that we had accomplished what He had sent us to Africa to do. Now, it was time to return to the Essex Church and help your dad and the church out."* They returned to the USA in July of 1991 at the end of their five–year appointment.

In September of 1991, we had special retirement and installation services in the Essex Church. Bishop Chester Wright served as the Master of Ceremonies, and a good number of our ministerial brethren were present. I officially passed the pastoral staff to my son.

Brother James Kilgore was the evening speaker. He had served as my son's pastor for the last two and a half years that my son attended Texas Bible College in Houston, Texas. My son looked to him as his second father. Once my son was officially installed as the new pastor in Essex, Maryland, I continued to assist him as Pastor Emeritus of the church.

After building two churches and filling the pastorate office for thirty-four years, it took some time for me to get adjusted to no longer being the pastor. From the beginning of my resignation, I always promoted my son to the congregation as their pastor. Some of the older saints still looked to both of us as pastor, and many times they would come to me with a need or problem.

My son appreciated me taking care of situations that could be solved without his involvement. However, all matter of church concerns I directed to my son who was now the senior pastor. If someone else had become the pastor, they would have probably felt threatened. But, my son knew that my concern was for the church and his spiritual welfare.

At the Maryland-DC District Conference in the spring of 1992, my son was elected by the brethren to once again serve on the district board as presbyter of our section. Before going to Kenya, he and Brother Ron Libby were both elected to serve as the first presbyters of the two new sections we added to our district. My son served almost seven years as presbyter before resigning to go on the foreign mission field of Kenya, East Africa.

It was a unique experience for both of us to be on the district board at the same time. For the past ten years, we have been serving together as District Honorary Board Members of the Maryland–D.C. District of the United Pentecostal Church International.

A Disturbing and Troubling Dream
October 7, 2005

Like most people, I have many dreams of which I remember only a small portion. But, a spiritual dream, a dream with a message, stays with me in minute detail. The following is a dream that caused me to experience a wide awakening.

The morning of October 7th, 2005 I awoke at 12:40 AM from a troubling dream. I dreamed that my wife was in the hospital on the bed, and I was sitting in a chair by her bedside. Someone else was in the room, but I was not aware of who that person was.

A woman appeared at the door dressed in a long black dress or more like a robe with a six-inch-wide white stripe running down the front. I said, *"No! Go in Jesus' name!"* The woman turned and left for a short period of time; but, then, again she reappeared at the door. I said again, *"No! In Jesus' name, get out!"* This woman turned and left the room again. After a short span of time, this woman reappeared for the third time at the door and looked straight at me. It was a look that I, for some reason, could not resist, and I nodded my head at her.

She turned, looked at my wife, held forth both of her hands and said, *"Come with me."* My wife started to get out of bed when an amazing thing happened. There appeared to be two bodies of my wife. One body that was very lively began rising without seemingly stepping on the floor and joined this woman. Together, they both disappeared. The other body laid back down with her head falling sideways off the bed. When I reached out to her from my chair at the bedside, it was as though my wife's life was gone. I shouted, *"No!"* Then, I woke up from my dream.

Troubled mind and spirit,
Doctor Ralph J. McIntyre

For some time, I could not find an answer to this dream, in which this woman in black appeared at the door three different times. I realized that a black garment is usually mentally associated with death, but I was in a deep ponder concerning the front of her robe with the white stripe, which I thought represented life.

Three weeks after having this dream, my wife suddenly became almost helpless. She could not get out of bed nor stand without my assistance. She had to be placed in a wheelchair and transported to the bathroom, dining room, etc. I had to help feed her, because she would drop most of her food. My wife could not bathe nor dress herself, because she had lost all use of her right hand and arm and had very little use of her left hand.

Due to my wife's condition, her body was very sore. I figured out a way to properly bathe and dress my wife that was almost painless. This condition had been most humiliating for her, but we both were very thankful that God had given me the strength and ability to care for her.

My wife had beautiful long uncut hair, which had now become a real challenge to keep done. She said to me, *"I don't know what I am going to do with my hair, I am not able to care for it any longer."* Every morning, she would roll and comb her hair. I said, *"I will fix it for you."* She said, *"You will fix my hair for me?"* I said, *"Yes."* I fixed her hair upon her head, and held the mirror up for her to take a look. After a moment, she said, *"That is not bad."*

I came to an understanding of my dream to mean that part of my wife died, and the other part still lived. We are both so very thankful that this sickness did not destroy nor affect her mind nor her kind and loving ways.

Approximately three months later on February 1st, 2006, Doctor Howard Goldman told me to call an ambulance and transport my wife to the hospital, where she spent six days. After undergoing a number of tests, my wife was sent for an MRI. The results of the MRI showed that her severe arthritis was heavily pressing the bones in her neck and squeezing against her spinal cord. Doctor Goldman and others wanted my wife to have surgery immediately, so he arranged for the neurosurgeon to observe her and give his opinion.

After the neurosurgeon came, he was very open and up-front stating that the problem was in the small bone in my wife's neck, where he had no room for error. Her fragile bones were not in her favor. His statement was that if we desired, he would perform the surgery with the understanding that she may become totally paralyzed or even die from this surgery.

My son asked the neurosurgeon, *"If this was your mother, what would you do?"* His reply was, *"That is a hard question. I would probably opt not to have the surgery."* My wife's body was in such a weakened state that she felt she could not survive the surgery and recovery therapy, so she refused to have it, which our whole family totally agreed with that decision.

From the hospital, my wife was sent to rehab, where she spent almost five weeks. They were able to help her learn to use a walker to move herself in a limited way to get around in the house; but, some of the time, she still had to have help in rising up from a sitting position. She, also, learned to feed herself with some difficulty using her left hand with a spoon fitted with a large foam handle. This lasted for a short period of time until she finally lost all use of her hands and had to be fed.

The other part of the dream, where she seemed to leave her body without her feet touching the floor, became clear to me, also. The bottom of my wife's feet was swollen and puffy, and she stated that she felt like she was walking on air without touching the floor. I never felt led to reveal my dream to my wife. I definitely believe this dream came from the Lord.

After arriving home from rehab, a therapist came to our home three times a week for my wife. Another lady, also, came to our home to bathe my wife twice a week for four weeks. My wife had an ulcer on her ankle that refused to heal; therefore, a nurse came to our home three days a week to dress her ankle. I told them that I could dress my wife's ankle as good as they were doing. From that point on, the nurse then started coming to our house only one day a week.

We had a number of wonderful ladies in our church family who willingly offered to assist us in any way possible. They were so kind, and we deeply appreciated their offers, but we were able to do fine on our own.

My wife was a private person, and for some time she had a fear of having to be placed in an assisted–living home. My wife felt comfortable with my care and, thankfully, God gave me the strength and desire to fully and lovingly take care of her. During our life together, the Lord always gave us the grace to face and endure many fiery trials. We were truly blessed!

On October 30th, 2009 a brother from the church by the name of David Toft brought us our dinner. I requested for him to please stay and eat with us. A short time later my wife's speech and words became very thick. Brother Toft and I prayed for her, but I knew something was wrong, and I said, *"I believe my wife is dehydrated."*

I informed her that she needed help that I was not able to give her. I really did not want to take her to the hospital, because she had told me earlier that if she went to the hospital, she would not come home. I knew she really did not want to go to the hospital.

That very day our son had agreed to teach a class in high school as a substitute teacher. I called him and said, *"Son, please come to our house as soon as school is over, because your mother is having a problem. I might have to take her to the hospital."*

When my son arrived, he explained to his mother that we did not want her to have to go to the hospital, but she needed medical treatment that neither one of us could give her, and we would really feel bad if something happened without us trying to get her the help she needed. She agreed to go, so we called the medics and they transferred her to the Franklin Square Hospital by ambulance.

When my wife was examined, she was found to be suffering from dehydration. After treatment, my wife began to talk normal and said that she was feeling much better. They were going to admit her, and I told her that I would stay there that night. She told me that she was feeling much better, and she begged me to please go home and get some rest. Finally, I consented. Early the next morning, I called the hospital to see how she was doing, and I was informed that she was in Intensive Care.

I got ready and left home for the hospital. When I arrived, I went directly to the Intensive Care Unit. I rang the bell, and a nurse came to the door and informed me that visiting hours did not begin until 12:00 noon.

When she started to close the door, I put my hand out and stopped her. I said, *"Listen, I am aware of visiting hours, but I brought my wife to the hospital last evening due to dehydration. After treatment, she began to feel good and persuaded me to go home and get some rest. Now, they have her in Intensive Care, and I want to know what is going on."*

The nurse said, *"Wait a minute!"* She checked with the doctor, and he said, *"Admit him."* I went to her station and saw her. Then, I learned that they had discovered a sepsis infection in her blood, and so far, they had not found an antibiotic to combat it.

Our son and his wife came immediately to the hospital. I called my daughter in Athens, Georgia, and she and her husband arrived in Baltimore, Maryland Sunday morning. Before long, our grandkids and whole immediate family were at the hospital. Beginning that morning, anyone (including the doctors) that visited my wife had to put on a gown and gloves.

On Monday evening our family was called into a conference room. Here, we received the heartbreaking news that they had done everything possible for my wife, but this was terminal and only a matter of time. The doctor asked if we wanted them to prolong her life if her heart stopped, such as, shocking her heart or putting her on a breathing machine. Both, our son and daughter, said that their mother would not want that, so we declined that offer.

We were informed that since there was no more that they could do, they would have to discharge her from the hospital on Wednesday. There was a representative of Hospice there in the hospital, and we went to see her. She was very nice, sympathetic and understanding. She explained in detail their services to us.

On Wednesday we went to the hospital to see my wife at their dinner time. Our daughter fed her mother, not knowing that she was feeding her mother her last meal. While Tawana, our granddaughter, and Karen, our daughter, were visiting with my wife, my wife looked at them and said, *"I want to go home."* Tawana said, *"I know, Mimi. We are trying to make arrangements to get you back home, so you can have hospice in your house."* My wife said, *"No, you don't understand. I'm not talking about that home."* Then, she pointed up and said, *"I'm talking about that home."*

Later, I went and checked to see when they were going to discharge my wife. They responded, *"This evening, the medics will arrive here around 5:00 PM."* I said, *"I was not aware of that. Where are they sending her?"* They said, *"Hospice."*

The medics arrived and placed my wife on the dolly. They asked me if I would like to ride in the ambulance with my wife, which I agreed to do so. It was approximately fifteen miles to the Stella Maris Hospice Facility.

My wife did not understand where she was being taken to, but I talked with her all the way trying to ease any fear or anxiety that she might experience. I explained that it was similar to a hospital, but much better. I told her that she would have her private room, and I would be with her.

When we arrived at Stella Maris, everyone was so helpful, kind and nice. When they got my wife comfortable in the bed, we were permitted to go in. A gentleman there asked me if I was going to stay with her through the night, and I replied, *"Yes!"* He said, *"I will get you a cot,"* and I was able to stay with my wife day and night for the nine days that she was there.

Wednesday was her last meal, because on Thursday morning when her breakfast arrived, the nurse tried to feed her, but after she put a bite in her mouth, it just laid there. The nurse had to remove it. She was not able to speak again after Wednesday night. I was informed that although she could not eat or talk, she could hear me. Therefore, I should continue to talk to her. The family could visit anytime day or night.

Between four and five o'clock each morning, I would kneel beside her bed, put my arm around her and pray. This seemed to be soothing to her. On Thursday, November 12th, 2009, my wife would not take her eyes off of me. If I moved out of her sight, she became very restless. One time Lynda, our daughter-in-law, said to me, *"Dad, mom is looking for you."* I moved within her view, and she became contented.

On Friday morning, November 13th, 2009, I was praying with her, and I said, *"Honey, I know that you are concerned and worried about me. I want you to know that you don't have to worry, because the Lord will take care of me. My trust is fully in Him. I know that you are tired, and you desire to go to your reward; therefore, I release you in order that you may go."*

When the nurse came in that morning, I said, *"There is a change in my wife this morning."* The nurse checked her with her stethoscope. Then, she looked up at me and nodded her head in agreement to my observation. All through that day, our children were there with my wife and me.

That evening at 6:25 PM, I was on my knees with my arm around my wife, when I felt her heart make a change. I said, *"Children, your mother is getting ready to leave us."* At 6:35 PM on this Friday, November 13th, 2009, she turned her head, drew a long breath and she was gone to her reward. On Thursday, November 19th, 2009, my wife was laid to rest at the Veterans Cemetery in Crownsville, Maryland at 3:00 PM.

After the services at the cemetery, we all gathered at Antioch, The Apostolic Church, pastored by Bishop Chester Wright. The ladies from this church prepared a wonderful meal, and everyone was invited to participate. God's people are so wonderful.

When we all departed, my family joined me back at my house. Eventually, everyone began to leave to return to their respective places. My son said, *"Dad, if you would like, Lynda and I will come over and stay with you."* I said, *"Son, I truly appreciate that, but honestly, I feel that I just need to be alone."*

Getting adjusted was truly a new experience for me. It just takes time and prayer. But, over time, the God we serve has a way of healing the hurt in the empty spot of the loss of a loved one, when we are confident that our loved one has departed to a place of magnificent glory that our Heavenly Father has prepared for those that love Him.

An Amazing Trip to Georgia

In May of 2010, I traveled to Athens, Georgia to spend some time with my daughter, Karen, and her husband, Pastor Steve Cole. I knew that I had a second cousin by the name of Judy Bandy that lived in the Atlanta, Georgia area. I had not seen Judy in several years. I was able to locate her phone number and, therefore, I called her. She was thrilled to hear from me.

On May 13th, 2010, my daughter and her husband were going on a trip concerning church business, which took them through the area in which Judy lived. I made an appointment with Judy, and my children dropped me off at her house to visit with her. I spent several hours with her.

From the age of six years old, Judy was plagued with the crippling disease of polio. An epidemic of this dreadful disease had broken out in the United States in the 1940's. This horrible disease had crippled Judy in both of her legs, causing her to wear leg braces and use crutches to walk.

Judy knew that I was a Christian minister; therefore, she began to ask me different questions concerning certain Scriptures. I soon discerned that Judy was very spiritually hungry. I said, *"Judy, would you like for me to give you a Bible study on the new spiritual birth?"* Judy said, *"Oh" yes, I would love it."* I gave Judy a rather lengthy Bible study. When

I concluded, Judy said, *"I have always wanted to be baptized, but due to my physical condition, I have never been able to."*

After the Bible study, Judy gave me a tour of her house which was rather large. In one room, I noticed that she had a big jacuzzi. When we returned to her living room, I asked Judy, *"Do you still desire to be baptized?"* Judy said, *"Oh yes, I would like to be baptized in Jesus' name and receive the Holy Ghost."* I said, *"Judy, your jacuzzi that you have in that room is a perfect baptismal tank. When my daughter and son-in-law return to pick me up, we can baptize you, then."* Judy said, *"I could never get in and out of that tub."* I said, *"Don't worry. We will get you in, and we will get you out."*

When my children returned, I explained to them about the wonderful Bible study that we had just concluded. They were thrilled! Pastor Steve Cole, then, talked to Judy. We all had a great prayer with her. My daughter ran water into the jacuzzi while Judy got dressed for baptism. When she was ready, she left her leg braces off and crawled from her bedroom to the jacuzzi room. We started to help her get into the jacuzzi, but she insisted on trying to get in herself, which she did without any trouble.

Pastor Steve Cole and I baptized her in the name of the Lord Jesus Christ for the remission of her sins. When she came up out of the water, she began thanking and praising the Lord. Her face began to shine. Suddenly, she wasn't speaking her mother tongue of English, but she was speaking in tongues as God baptized her with the Holy Ghost.

Church Relocation

I returned back to Baltimore after spending an awesome time in Georgia. For several months after the death of my wife,

I had remained at the church in Essex, Maryland that I had founded and pastored for twenty-six years.

In prayer, I felt that it would be best if I relocated to another place of worship. I felt strongly led by God to relocate to the Abundant Life Church pastored by Reverend David Reever. This church was approximately five miles from my home.

I called Pastor Reever and asked him how he would feel if I chose to attend his church. He said, *"Elder, you would have been welcome last week."* I cleared everything at the Life Center in Essex, Maryland with Pastor Scott Richardson, my grandson-in-law, whom I love dearly. Then, I made Abundant Life Church my home church in 2010.

Terry and Lynda McIntyre

Missionaries to the Fiji Islands

In April of 2010, Terry and Lynda attended the Veterans of Global Missions Retreat in Potosi, Missouri. Still having a burden for the foreign mission field, they talked to the Global Missions Director of the UPCI, Reverend Bruce Howell, about being willing to go anywhere in the world where there was a need on the AIM (Associates In Missions) program. Without hesitation, Brother Howell said, *"Fiji! We have no missionary there at this time and you could be a big help with the Bible College and your ministry in the various churches across those islands."* Brother Howell put them in touch with the Pacific Regional Director, Brother Richard Denny.

The next fourteen months they planned and sought support from various churches, friends and family to go to Fiji. In June of 2011, they departed for these islands. They have been doing this for the past nine consecutive years. Their stay each year is approximately six months (June–December). They have witnessed people being raised from the dead, paralyzed folks walking, many folks receiving the baptism of the Holy Ghost, many folks being baptized in water by immersion in the name of the Lord Jesus Christ and many other miracles that have taken place across these islands.

I mentioned earlier in this book about my military days during World War Two, which included me going to Tarawa in the Gilbert Islands located in the South Pacific. While in Fiji, my son had the privilege of ministering in Tarawa seventy-four years after I had been there. However, he came in a different military, the Army of the Lord, and saw people born again of the water and the Spirit.

While they are in Fiji, I spend several months with my daughter in Georgia. She and her husband treat me so well, and they go out of their way to accommodate me with anything they think I need or want.

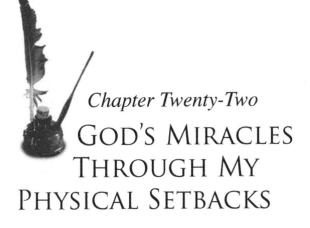

Chapter Twenty-Two

GOD'S MIRACLES THROUGH MY PHYSICAL SETBACKS

O n April 7th, 2016, I was admitted to St. Joseph Hospital with angina pain in my chest. An artery in the back of my heart was causing the discomfort. They said they could not put a stent in this artery, because it was too dangerous. The cardiologist asked me, *"Would you consider another open-heart surgery?"* I responded, *"No!"*

On Sunday evening, April 12th, the doctors came into my room and informed me that there was nothing else that they could do, and they had to discharge me. I said, *"I am still having those pains. What can I do?"* The doctor said, *"You will just have to take a nitro pill."*

On the next Thursday evening, I was in church. While the choir was singing, I stood up, raised my hands in worship and that pain left me. That has been four years ago, and I have not had any angina pain since.

On Sunday, July 30th, 2017, I was visiting Doctor Rohan Rengen and his family in Frederick, Maryland. His mother, Kay Lall, had become a member of our church in Essex, Maryland when he was only three years old. He became a medical doctor. His medical practice is in Frederick, Maryland.

He and his wife, Suneeta, had a new home built and requested for me to come on this Sunday to pray a prayer of blessing on their new home. My good friend from the Life Center in Essex, Maryland, Donald Parsons, volunteered to drive me to their home in Frederick. We had a wonderful afternoon.

However, when we were leaving their house, the sun was shining so brightly in my eyes that I missed a step and fell down hard on the concrete walkway. Both of my wrists were broken, my nose was broken and all of the roots of my upper teeth were broken. (The broken roots of my teeth were not discovered until later. When discovered, I had to have all of my upper teeth extracted).

When I fell, I blacked out. The 911 call for medics was immediately made by those that were there. Doctor Rohan Rengen packed ice on my nose to stop the bleeding. When the medics arrived, they worked on me for some time.

Doctor Rengen knocked on the ambulance door to ask them what was taking so long. They informed him that due to my serious injuries, medical history and advanced age of almost ninety-four years, I needed to be flown by a medevac helicopter to the University Hospital in Baltimore, Maryland. In a few minutes, the helicopter arrived, and I was taken on board. In approximately twenty minutes, we landed on the roof of the hospital.

Once at the hospital, they rolled the gurney inside to where several doctors and nurses gathered around me. I was examined, and they discovered along with the other injuries that there was bleeding on my brain. I was asked different questions.

Finally, a nurse asked if I had any relatives that she could contact. I said, *"I have a daughter, but she lives in Georgia."* At this time my son, Terry, and his wife, Lynda, were in the Fiji Islands as missionaries. Then, I said, *"I have a granddaughter that lives here in Maryland."* The nurse asked me if I knew her phone number, and I said, *"No."*

At this time I was in a semi–coma, but all of a sudden, a phone number popped into my mind. I said, *"Wait! Try this number."* In moments, the nurse came in and said, *"We got in touch with your granddaughter, and she is on her way here."* God surely had to reveal that number to me, because her number is a hard number to remember and one that I don't call often.

When my granddaughter, Tawana Richardson, arrived, the doctors told her that they might have to operate on my head to stop the bleeding. My granddaughter told them that she did not feel comfortable with that. She and her husband, Reverend Scott Richardson, prayed for me.

They took another cat scan of my brain. When they came back, they told my granddaughter that the bleeding had stopped, the blood was fading and surgery was not now necessary. That was great news! Thank God for answering their prayers! I was in the hospital four days. Then, I was transferred to Oakwood Rehab in Middle River, Maryland, where I spent six weeks.

After my discharge from Rehab, my daughter, Karen, and her husband, Reverend Steve Cole, had driven up from Athens, Georgia, to take me home with them for several weeks. I am thankful and blessed that I have children and grandchildren that love and care for me. I received royal treatment by my children and by the congregation of the First Pentecostal Church of Athens, Georgia.

After my visit, I returned to Baltimore, and it was very good to be back in the meetings at Abundant Life Church. The people were very glad to see me, and it was surely good for me to be able to be back in worship with all of them. I am privileged to sit under this man of God, Pastor David Reever. He, his family and the church body have accepted me with open arms. They love and honor me very highly. Thank God for Abundant Life Church of Baltimore, Maryland.

Raised Back to Life

On Sunday morning, September 16, 2018, there was a congregation of three hundred attendees or more at Abundant Life Church. The choir and all the congregation were worshiping together in song. I began to feel a tight pressure in my chest and thought that it was angina pain. I proceeded to place a nitro tablet under my tongue. It seemed, as though, all of the pressure went to my head. I immediately sat down. Then, everything became bright, and I passed out. Brother Donnie Martin, who was sitting beside me, thought I had fallen asleep. He tried to wake me and found out that I was not asleep.

Pastor Reever had just stepped up to the pulpit to deliver his message, when he saw me and said, *"I need a doctor and nurse up front right now."* Doctor Pauline Daley and Nurse Emiko Chase responded immediately. Doctor Daley checked me and stated, *"He has no pulse or heartbeat."* At that point, Nurse Chase performed CPR on me, which broke my ribs. The medics were called.

Brother Dave Price was concerned that the medics would have a difficult time finding the location of the church. So, he immediately left the sanctuary and ran a long distance to the main road, which was Philadelphia Road. Just as he arrived at this main road, he saw the emergency vehicle coming at a fast rate of speed. Knowing that the driver was going to drive past the entrance to the church, Brother Price ran out into the street waving his arms for the driver to stop. When he stopped, Brother Price directed him to the church sanctuary where I was still unresponsive.

The congregation was earnestly praying in the Spirit. God's presence filled that sanctuary. When the medics arrived, they placed pads on my chest and back to shock my heart. Just before they began the heart shock treatment, Doctor Daley spoke up and said, *"I feel a pulse."* My heart began to function once again. The medics transferred me to the hospital. Later, the medics came to check on me and said, *"Those people in that church were really praying for you, but we could not under-stand a word that they were saying."*

On Monday my cardiologist, Doctor Jeffrey Brown, came to my room and stated, *"Reverend, this was not your heart. It was a reaction of the nitro tablet and acid reflux."* This reac-tion actually caused my heart to stop. This was a great relief to know. Doctor Brown cautioned me to never take the nitro tablet unless I knew the problem was definitely my heart.

The next day I was discharged from the hospital. Thankfully, I have not had a recurrence of this problem. Only God can give life, and by extending mine, there is evidently another purpose He has for me on this earth. My prayers are that I will always be sensitive to His Spirit and hear His voice when He speaks to my spirit.

Chapter Twenty-Three
CONCLUSION

I'm thankful for the truth and the true church that is in touch with God. Multitudes join a religious body and settle it in their mind that they are alright, but so many are caught up in false gods and false religions. You must realize that there is so much deceit in the world. The only way that you can find the right way is to pray earnestly and sincerely and read from the book of life, the Holy Bible, with an open mind and heart until you hear the voice of God. He will lead you right. Romans 8:14 (KJV) states *"For as many as are led by the Spirit of God, they are the sons of God."*

Jesus said that He is coming back, and whether you believe it or not, He is coming back for a people that have made themselves ready without spot or blemish of the filth of this world. We are seeing many signs that Jesus said would appear prior to His return.

During the time I spent refreshing my mind concerning all of my days in which God has granted me on His created earth, I gained a renewed understanding of my purpose in life. As humans, it is our nature to desire that all things that we face will be pleasant without any adverse or negative situations. If Adam had not disobeyed God, this could have been. Satan would not have become the god of this world blinding minds of unbelievers.

From searching the past, I recalled so many things that God had brought me through. I finally arrived with the understanding that I was now serving the same God that Apostle Paul served, when God reminded him in I Corinthians 12:9 (KJV), *"My grace is sufficient for thee; for my strength is made perfect in weakness. Most gladly therefore will I rather glory in my infirmities, that the power of Christ may rest upon me."* I came to the realization that these adverse experiences in my life actually were preparing me for the day my life would be totally changed.

So many times, during my life, I was staring death straight in the face. To some people, my life may have looked hopeless, but God looks upon the heart and sees things differently. He saw what no natural eye could see. He saw the hunger in my heart and, in His due time, He moved and changed me. If He can change me, He can change anyone.

I would plead with any person that has never had a transforming life experience with God to please study the Scriptures and obey them. They are God's Word and powerful enough to completely change any individual on the face of the earth. Everyone has experienced the physical birth, in which all are born into sin. However, to please God and be ready when He returns to earth, you must experience the spiritual birth.

In the book of John, Jesus explained to Nicodemus about the new birth and its necessity to enter into God's Kingdom. We read about this account in John 3:5 (KJV) where Jesus declared, *"Verily, verily, I say unto thee, except a man be born of water and of the Spirit, he cannot enter into the kingdom of God."*

When I experienced being born again of water and the Spirit, I found out that this experience caused the same Spirit that raised Jesus from the dead to take its abode within me and make me alive spiritually. Apostle Paul wrote about this to the church at Rome and stated, *"But if the Spirit of Him that raised up Jesus from the dead dwell in you, He that raised up Christ from the dead shall also quicken your mortal bodies by His Spirit that dwelleth in you* (Romans 8:11 KJV).

Paul, also, wrote to the church at Corinth in I Corinthians 3:16 (KJV) and said, *"Know ye not that ye are the temple of God, and that the Spirit of God dwelleth in you?"* This new birth experience is not just a change of mind, but a miraculous change of heart that only God can perform on an individual that truly "hungers and thirsts" after Him.

Marquis *Who's Who in Religion* is a book that chronicles the lives of today's religious leaders. Some of these leaders, no doubt, are sincere in their walk with God while others, perhaps, follow afar off. Among all of these, I was honored and privileged to be listed in this renown book's Fourth Edition for the year 1992–1993.

However, as the world continues to make advancements in the fields of mathematics, science, technology, etc. in improving our physical lives, it is much more important to advance in not only religion, but in true salvation for the improvement of our spiritual lives. This is especially true as we move into the twentieth year of the twenty-first century. The bottom line is God's Word is absolute truth and will be the only thing standing when heaven and earth passes away (Matthew 24:35 KJV).

My prayer and heart's desire for everyone that takes the time to give my book a sincere perusal is that they will find strength and a hope for their own lives and their loved ones. Jesus loves all souls. He is not prejudiced, racial, partial or a respecter of persons. What God has done for me is available to whomsoever will turn unto Him in full faith. God enrobed or manifested Himself in flesh as the Son of God to save lost humanity.

Although not everyone will follow and obey the Lord, Apostle Peter enlightens us to the fact that God's will is for no one to perish. He stated, *"...Not willing that any should perish, but that all should come to repentance"* (II Peter 3:9 KJV). But, if you refuse Him, He will refuse you.

May God's blessings be with you and guide you through your daily life, and when God calls your name in eternity, He will say to you, *"Well done, good and faithful servant! Enter thou into the joy of thy Lord!"* (Matthew 25:23 KJV)

**Dr. Ralph McIntyre's 80th Birthday with His Wife, Frances
Their Children, Grand-children and Great-grandchildren
(Four Generations)**

MIRACULOUSLY CHANGED

I came into this world, by the hands of a midwife,
She lightly gave me a smack, and I sprung to life;
I was a healthy boy, which made my parents glad,
Most folks that saw me said I looked like my dad.

My mom and dad were great, sometimes very funny,
We were not poor people, we just didn't have money;
At my age seven on Christmas morn, dad had passed away,
Mother could not support us, with her we could not stay.

To lose both parents at once is truly a tragedy for sure,
Without mom and dad's care, the world can easily lure;
As I matured in age, I plunged very deep into sin,
I was sick of life, but to change I knew not how to begin.

I met and married a very innocent and lovely girl,
Her desires were heavenly, but mine were of the world;
World War Two shattered my nerves, I leaned on strong drink,
Our family was almost destroyed, my ship was about to sink.

In a vision I was shown the roaring fires of hell,
The things I saw were horrible, very hard for me to tell;
Then I found myself, lifted high into the sky,
Satan's chain was broken, I no longer believed his lie.

I was a woeful sinner, and my life was on display,
But Jesus' love miraculously delivered me that day;
I had joined the losing team, no way for me to win,
But a new life was then granted, for me to enter in.

Conclusion

From that day I began, knocking on heaven's door
Truly, my heart was sick, and my soul was very sore;
The Holy Spirit undergirded, and helped me to stand,
And, from that day forth, I became a brand-new man.

I was such a debtor, and no way to pay the fee,
But Calvary's blood paid my debt, now I am free;
No longer do I have to hang my head in shame,
I am free from my woeful life I now wear Jesus' name.

The sayings in this poem are all so very true,
I am so thankful for all the Lord brought me through;
Jesus is now and will forever be my all in all,
I'm so gloriously blessed since I answered His call.

—-Dr. Ralph Jackson McIntyre (clergy)
(composed on February 12, 2012)

CPSIA information can be obtained
at www.ICGtesting.com
Printed in the USA
LVHW011351130920
665854LV00002B/2